HIT YOUR RESTART BUTTON

BUTTON

HOW TO REINVENT YOURSELF AND START LIVING A ZERO LIMITS LIFE

RANJAN KUMAR

ISBN 978-1-63745-731-3

To my kids Sanjitha and Ishan

To the all-pervading spirit of universal life

Contents

Preface

Do you see yourself crushed between your day job and personal dreams? Does fulfillment seem an unrealistic dream now? Do you feel guilty that you aren't able to present your best self these days to your kids, family and loved ones?

Then I have some good news for you...

As you read every word here, you will be amazed how simple it is to reinvent yourself, face the fast-changing world boldly and live a fulfilled life, without leaving your day job and in less than 60 minutes a day.

According to Albert Bandura, the David Starr Jordan Professor Emeritus of Social Science Psychology at Stanford University, people are naturally self-organizing, proactive, self-reflecting and self-regulating, not just reactive organisms shaped by environmental forces or driven by internal impulses.

He presented the perspective on how a person's attitude, abilities, and cognitive skills constitute his self-system. This system plays a crucial role in how we perceive our circumstances and respond to them.

Hit Your Restart Button is here to help you build such a powerful self-system which can help you develop all the qualities of an authentic self-leader and lead a life inside-out – a life of self-reliance, self-efficacy, and natural self-confidence. All in all it's going to help you explore the art of authentic self leadership.

If you've led an adventurous life so far chasing BIG goals, creating and meeting deadlines, striving for a balance between family and work, you must already be awaiting the right opportunity to rekindle your spirit and take your next shot at life.

If you have been aiming at big goals but somehow feel confused about your real purpose, and have been swinging between moments of success and hollowness in your gut, you have already whipped yourself hard, and know deep down that you haven't got what you actually had set out for.

If you have often felt inadequate in your skills, talents and abilities, then you might also have gone through the need to be special or the best or unique in your identity. You might have suffered the fear of failure, guilt about success, or might have felt like a fraud within saying, "I must not fail", "I feel like a fake", or "I just got lucky".

If all of this sounds familiar, you might also have been in denial of your ability and might have discounted praise unconsciously on most occasions.

Now let me tell you the truth: you are not alone. In fact, most high-achievers have been through such states. For a confession, I too have been through all such states and feelings for years. But let me also tell you with the same conviction, "You don't have to be stuck there. You don't have to suffer 'not-enoughness' until you become a captive of the pattern. There is a way out. And it goes inward."

Tried and failed? Let me tell you something: The question is not about your ability. What matters is your willingness. If you're willing to step into your greatness and create a life of choice, you are at your destination.

Welcome!

I grew up exploring all the possible ways I could succeed in living my dream because my parents were busy helping me prepare for 'survival'. BIG dreams were only part of my sleep. It wasn't that they didn't intend to help me 'thrive'. They just didn't know how to.

Random choices became my way of life. Accidental turns were the only things triggering my future. Emotional ups and downs were the only roller-coaster rides I had fun with until 30.

In spite of my early exposure to the energy therapies such as pranic-healing, reiki, yoga, meditation, hypnotism, and the subconscious way of creating a future of choice, I still felt lost.

What I realized very late in life was that I was not living my story. I woke up to fact that I had to do something with all that I had learnt. But the roots of my past beliefs had already penetrated so deep that they had merged with the cells in my body. I discovered that I had to create and follow a system that could help me live up to my full potential.

I got down to getting my hands dirty, started taking bold decisions, took criticism in the stride, and kept on keeping on.

'Did the situations change?' 'Perhaps, no.'

'Did I improve?' 'You bet!'

It's only when I realized that it's not the destination that matters, and that what matters is only and only progress, I started living my story. Remember it's not the goal that changes your life; it's the process that transforms you.

Yes, you need a purpose to stick to your story and drive you superfast. But there is a lot to the story than just the purpose.

Let me start by sharing the truth that it's possible to restart at any point in life, start from scratch, make a fresh beginning and make a difference. That's exactly what authentic self leadership is all about.

Answer yourself: How would your life be different if you could turn your dreams real? How would it help your family and loved ones? What's the cost you are paying for being stuck?

Imagine that at age 75 you are telling your life story to a grandchild. What would you like to be able to tell him/her about how you responded to your challenges?

Put your palm on your chest and feel your body responding. Open your inner ears and listen to your soul. Envision your future self and ask, "Where would you have me go?" and "What would you have me do?"

Ask yourself in silence, "What will you lose if you don't do something about personal transformation. Who all will suffer if you don't step ahead and embrace change? What's at stake?"

Confession: It wasn't my 'ability' that blocked my path of progress but was my lack of 'willingness' to change. My question to you is, "Are you willing to do what it takes to live your dream?" If you hear a yes from inside, you are ready for the journey.

Now that you're ready to give your life a purpose, you have the road map in your hands. All you need to do is to commit yourself to read this book, apply the wisdom, chalk out a plan and ACT on it.

This book takes cue from Robert Kiyosaki's words in The Business of The 21st Century in which he speaks about how building and then losing a worldwide business gave him real-world education that ultimately made him rich. And that it was education which set him free.

I asked myself, "Which education?

And got the answer from his own words where he confesses that the most important things he learned were not about business or money – they were about him.

This book is all about reinventing the authentic you.

It's more about who you become than what you do.

It is no accident that you picked up this book. Perhaps, it is an act of the most powerful creative force that we meet in the pages inside.

You are not alone. The desire to re-invent is natural because we have a natural instinct for breakthrough innovations. Look around and you will see the impact in everything you come across. Don't you agree we would have perished without this innate desire to reinvent ourselves?

It's so strong that we have re-invented ourselves umpteen times. We have aced it so well that we have conquered the planet and are going beyond!

The only blind spot left for you to conquer is you.

You know what I mean, don't you?

Hit Your Restart Button is going to be the light-house you can rely upon henceforth to build an unconquerable mindset because you certainly deserve what you are made for. The moment you do it, you start living by choice.

At the same time, I want to agree with the British journalist Bryan Appleyard's argument in his book How to Live Forever or Die Trying that you might not be able to stretch or reinvent your personality indefinitely. You are intelligent enough to know that there is a natural phase in life when your desire to reinvent yourself is at its peak.

You are at a point when you have resources million fold what you had a decade ago. Still you can feel the rising dissatisfaction in our lives. What could be causing it?

See around once and you will see wounded souls chasing something elusive. People devastated in personal and professional lives and hearts are screaming for peace and love. World-class performers are committing suicides and teens are giving in to stress.

Tell me, "What does this dissatisfaction point at?"

If you ask me, "It's lack of authentic self leadership."

Dig deeper and you'll see that in spite of thousands of world-class institutions mushrooming across; surveys still point at the lack of much-desired personal skills and professional skills.

On the opposite, world is witnessing a never before seen participation of the youth in the greatest causes. In a mysterious way 'indifference' has made friends with 'active citizenship'.

Social media has emerged as a newer dimension of participation. The truth is that most of the times it leaves you with only a feel of participation than giving you actual results. In one way or the other, we have seen the upsurge of youth participation.

The question is, "What does this signify?"

World is brimming with a new hope for revival through the power of youthful energy. Don't you see it coming forward and pushing on towards a rebirth?

Now stop for a moment and ask yourself, "Who's going to lead this change?"

"Only authentic self-leaders."

The active involvement of the youth exposes the burning desire to look on the brighter side. Once you decide to join in and be part of this change-leading generation you will be the driving force behind this major shift!

Wondering how? Let' see.

We can dramatically halve the period of transition by helping our youth to make meaning, and lead a purpose-driven life. And this is possible only by empowering them with the art of authentic self leadership.

After all, who would be risking life by boarding a rudderless ship?

Envision a world filled with youth - self-reliant, sensible, and purpose driven.

Wouldn't this mean a BIG change for us?

What then is the best way to spark the process?

This book will help you figure it out. It doesn't matter who you are and what background you come from; try the ideas to get two of your crucial questions answered:

1. What's the mindset you need to become a self-leader?

2. What's the simple structure to turn it real?

What to Expect From this Book?

In the first part "The Authentic Self Leadership Mindset Uncovered" you get the proven principles, attitudes and habits of thinking you must build to grow as a self-leader.

I really wish I could be more specific but I can't because you will want to feel the thrill first-hand!

The companion copy (the second part) of this book "You.2 – A Crash Course in Authentic Self Leadership" is where the rubber meets the road. You get a backdoor entry to your success-mindset. Whether you are a 'seeker' or a 'change-maker', it presents you the easy structure you can put to use and bring about the desired transformation. Use this part as your secret door to rediscover life!

A friend of mine recently said that with almost any book he picked up these days a question popped up in his head, "Will this book go beyond motivation?",

The answer to you my friend is, "Hell to the yes it will!"

See it for yourself. Because that's the only way you get exposed to life's naked truths, uncensored. The only way you can conquer reality and live your authentic self is by exploring the truths by taking action. You become successful when you're willing to push yourself to the breaking point – and then go beyond!

Once you finish reading this book and act on the thoughts, you will surprise yourself with the shift you will see. All you need to do now is Hit Your Restart Button and launch yourself!

Man, I am going to EXPLODE!

Let's go for it!

-Ranjan Kumar

Acknowledgements

I thank you first for accepting me into your mission of becoming a self-leader. I thank my parents and two wonderful kids. You give me enough space to be myself. I thank my friends. You put trust in me and helped me further my cause. Thanks to all who challenged my beliefs, which in turn challenged me to make meaning in life.

I extend my pranams to H. H. Srimad Swami Sri Ranganathanandaji [Ex-International President; Sri Ramakrishna Math and Mission Order] who gave me mantra deeksha (Spiritual Initiation) and gave me a glimpse of the invisible. I thank my pranic healing masters. Words fail me even as I thank my Reiki Masters Late. Sri Chandramouli and Smt C. Sowmya who gave me some awe-inspiring experiences. I thank Master Sarvari for initiating me in Master CVV's path of meditation.

I thank Junior Chamber International – India where I got to explore the transformational trainer within. I acknowledge with gratitude the timely suggestions and consistent cooperation from all my fellow speakers and trainers across India. I thank all the participants of my talks and workshops as well as my life-coaching clients who helped me grow along with them.

And if your mind is still hooked on the cover page then I owe a lot to Dr. Apta – International Branding Strategist (www.merogdesign.com) for his contribution. And above all, I thank the spirit of universal transformation for choosing me as an instrument of change.

-Ranjan Kumar

CHAPTER ONE

INTRODUCTION – HOW YOU CAN TURN A SUPERHUMAN?

"IT IS THE COWARD AND THE FOOL who say, "This is my fate." But it is the strong man who stands up and says, "I will make my fate," declared Swami Vivekananda to the world.

It's this I am going to talk to you about today.

At some time you must have given in to the pressures of life and taken a short cut or done something badly. You must have explored all the possible ways to succeed in creating success in your career, family, and other categories of your choice.

You might have led a corporate life chasing goals tirelessly, meeting deadlines, and working hard to make ends meet. You might also have survived the emotional turmoil of a break up or being broke. You might have lost hope in future due to an unexpected loss of a loved one, or are just recovering from the emotional roller-coaster ride of a terrible divorce. You might have been braving inclement weather in your personal life as a single parent, or might have just decided to revoke the decision of ending your life. I don't know what your story is, but I have something to ask you.

What is a story without a conflict?

And what is life without challenges?

Donald Miller in his book A Million Miles In A Thousand Years defines a story as a character who wants something, and overcomes conflict to get it.

Isn't that who we are and what we are doing?

I know why you are here. You are here because you have tried all the possible ways to be bold and face all the obstacles life at you. You have done enough to bounce back and create a new life. But each time you made a comeback, life threw a fresh barrage of challenges upon you to deal with. And you found yourself submerged under the avalanche of new challenges, gasping for a fresh lease of life.

You had a dream when you began in your career, but seem have to have lost your way and now see yourself crushed between your dream-life and your livelihood.

While you are disappointed at many things in life, you want to make a fresh beginning because somehow you feel that there's something you can do about your mindset. You know deep down there's something right about you but don't know why it doesn't click.

You might have changed over half-a-dozen careers not knowing what your real call is. You might have suffered the pain of break ups in spite of true love, or might be feeling lonely without a single friend in spite of your positive attitude.

On the outside you might have been perceived as a confident, dynamic and successful person while on the inside you can hear yourself crying of loneliness in your heart.

I don't know what your story is, but I know one thing for sure.

You are here because you decided to give one more shot at life. You are here because you decided to look within for answers. You are here because you are chosen to become a self-leader.

I am an ordinary guy who was penniless and had started in 1998 as an attendant in a PCO (Public Call Office) in Rayagada, Odisha, India. The only things left for me to feed on from when my father had enough to spare for me were a few books on inner transformation.

Most of them were books from the likes of OSHO, Sri Aurobindo, Shakti Gawain, Barbara Ann Brenan, Swami Vivekananda, Theosophical Society of India, Ramana Maharshi, J. Krishnamurthy, Robert Schuller, and a slew of transformational leaders, gurus, authors, and organizations which helped me get a glimpse of life beyond the physical dimension.

I kept working my way up through jobs like being a receptionist at a medical diagnostic center and a hotel to make ends meet. But that was barely enough for a meal a day for my family. I and my father kept sweating and laboring hard to manage 3 meals a day.

At one point in the year 1999, we went so broke we couldn't manage to have enough for lunch for about a month, and had to survive on a liquid diet cheap enough for us to buy, and water, which we had abundantly.

I would get rupees 3/- worth of road-side fried-rice as my evening snack to appease my appetite while my mother would make some tea for me to help me keep going till dinner time.

Often I would cry gazing at the stars in the sky as if they were to answer my unasked questions. I would not accept what I was going through and found it difficult to accept the reality.

Finally, I decided to give up on life. I lost my faith in the future and thought of my life as no better than that of a bug. So what else could give me instant relief? The easiest way of getting relieved from this pain was to sit on a railway track and let the oncoming train to do the rest for me.

Or to leave my family once again (details of a previous attempt is given in a forthcoming chapter) in the name of spirituality and join a monk order of any spiritual order. This time the purpose was to escape the grind.

One fine morning, I took a train to Visakhapatnam, a city about 180 kilometers far, and joined as a monk in the Sri Ramakrishna Mission by afternoon. For about 4 hours, life was better and everything looked bright. At least I had a spiritual mask on to cover my story.

At about 7 P.M, I could hear my inner voice whispering something to me. In just a few minutes the voice grew loud enough demanding my attention. I started cursing myself to have run away from the battle and began holding myself accountable for having deserted my parents with no clue whatsoever. The pain grew unbearably intense and I was exploding with guilt. Here I was in the marshy terrain of confusion without any idea whatsoever.

But what else could I do? Life had turned miserable. I felt so helpless and coward within I hung my head in shame. And then it struck me that I had hit rock bottom. I heard my inner voice say, "This is the worst that could've happened. You don't want to put your parents' life at stake to pacify the coward in you. How far and how long do you think you can run? Life will catch up on you anytime."

I saw myself being nudged upwards by an invisible force and I decided to do something immediately.

I decided I am not going to run anymore. Not at least to escape the challenges life threw upon me. But I also decided NOT go back into the life of a bug either.

I chose to get crushed by the challenges than by the oncoming train. I decided to go back home but this time it would be a different me.

I decided I am not going to play a mute spectator anymore, get back in the driver's seat, take control, and start over. I am the same ordinary guy, but now a bestselling author, transformational speaker and coach, outstanding trainer awardee and a proud father of two lovely kids now.

All this happened because I did something that transformed my life. I worked on my mindset and woke up the self-leader within.

Did life stop throwing challenges? Nope.

Rather, I grew stronger to face them and deal with them mentally. More importantly, I mastered the art of authentic self leadership. This is exactly what I am going to share with you in the pages inside.

Let's come back to you.

Wish you could live it all over again? Wish you could connect with your call again? Wish you could explore the self-leader within?

I promise you will be able to do it once you finish reading this book. I know it's a very bold statement to make but I take it as a challenge to help you discover your fullest potential. I don't say I will be able to do it for you. Nobody can do it for someone else. But if you've reached this far, I trust you are here on purpose and that we can do it together. Agree?

Hope you have realized now that your dreams won't work until they are based on a solid structure– you. On the other hand, the very reason you want to live your dream is to expand your capacity and to go beyond the limits.

Before you take your major leap, there are a few questions you need to find answers for. Because all that would stop you from making progress in your transformation will mostly be the unanswered questions which we tend to ignore. And the best way to ensure progress would be to get your path cleared.

Ready to quell the fidgety monkey in your mind?

Turn the page...

CHAPTER TWO

CLEAR YOUR INNER BARRICADES

What if I told it's absolutely possible to "Ctrl + Z" and "Ctrl + Y" your life the way you want to do it. And that it's all possible when you stick to the step-by-step plan I am going to give you here to radically reinvent yourself and start living a zero limits life.

You might be a student, an employee, a boss, a teacher, a trainer, a public speaker, a doctor, an entrepreneur, or a self-growth freak like me. What I just want you to know is that as you focus on every word, you will discover how you can hit your restart button, start from scratch, and become what you CAN at the push of a button!

Ready? Here we go.

You probably have already heard about a great number of people who have created an extraordinary life for themselves. The single most important thing they all wanted us to believe was: we are beyond what we permit ourselves to be. The fact that you chose to read this book is the unarguable proof that you deserve to live BIG!

Now here's something important to prime your mind: You can do it regardless of who you are, where you are from, and what your story is.

Ever wondered how they made themselves sooo BIG?

Let me share something crucial: the major cause of success or failure, in most cases, is the kind of questions we ask ourselves.

Yes, the trick that changed the way I began to see change in life – (oops, am I already giving the game away?!) is that I changed the questions I asked myself.

Now that I've already revealed the first step, let me open up to you fully. Years ago, I accidentally stumbled upon a question that changed the way I looked at life. Let me help you jumpstart your journey in the same manner.

Don't curse me if you experience a crazy shift within, way beyond your wildest dreams. Just kidding! What else would you expect from me?

WARNING: this system works best only when you apply it with an open mind. Feel free to give it a try.

First of all, let me see if you qualify for the trip.

Tell me, "Who decides your fate?"

Is it your DNA? Your parents? Your surroundings? Your circumstances? Your doctor? Your astrologer? Or your friends?

Listen. The question is "Who decides your fate?"

In other words, "Who's calling the shots in YOUR life?" Your family, your job, your coach, the economy, or something else?

Try answering one more, "What's directing your next step?"

If your mind is trying hard to point at anything but you, you've got the right book in your palms.

While you respond to the questions, you have already kicked off the game of uncovering the most powerful person you will ever know - YOU.

Here's a truth: Although I've been devouring gazillion of books for over a zillion years, there has been no better teacher than personal experience. Agree?

And that's exactly what makes this life-changing manual special. It's authentic and original because it's the result of all that I have personally gone through, and all that has helped me rise from desperation to fulfillment.

The good news is that I am going to give away every bit of it in this transformational manual. What's more, you could save years of toil. Imagine!

You are going to unravel some plain universal truths that will change your life like day and night. And I am quite sure you won't be the same person once you finish this book and put into practice each step presented here.

You will be BETTER. It's a promise.

Now pay attention.

Way back when I was 11 years old, I was a big fan of Bollywood movies. For a number of years, I grew up watching at least one every day. If you know Bollywood, you know they portray their hero as rough, tough, and doughty, always winning against incredible odds, and one with superhuman abilities – a SUPERHERO.

Believe it or not, they can do just about anything. Like most Indian children, I too was enthralled looking at such jaw-dropping heroism. If you know Bollywood closely, you will agree that the hero has a macho look in his eyes with a can-do-everything attitude.

Like most children of my age, I would carry these images in my memory and fantasize about becoming like them – a SUPERHERO.

The next thing that impressed me deeply was the magical powers of Lord Hanuman. I would never miss an episode of the 1987 television series based on the Indian epic Ramayana. In this, Lord Hanuman could fly across the oceans covering miles, and magically appear and disappear at will. I was awed at his marvelous superhuman feats.

Inside, a question would bug me always. Unable to resist it anymore, I once rushed to my dad and asked innocently, "What's the secret of his power?" "Only gifted people get such powers. They are God -given," answered my dad absently, his attention absorbed by the tobacco in his palms.

"As if he knows it firsthand," I muttered to myself.

But this was enough to peg out a limiting belief in my mind that the universe was biased towards a chosen few.

"How unfair!" I thought.

I still vividly remember how I used to childishly lock myself in a dimly lit bedroom-cum-dining-cum-study room and pray Lord Hanuman to appear and grant me powers similar to his.

And here's what I realized years later.

May be it's true that only a few gifted people can accomplish some magical feats, but there is some good news: if they have got those powers, we too have got some!

Let's see how.

Studies have proved that energy can neither be created nor destroyed. And if it is the same energy that exists everywhere, then what's available to someone is also available to you. Think.

Don't believe me, believe yourself. Join me to check out...

...How You Too Can Create Magic?

Universe has given us all the raw material. It has also given us free access to the device that manufactures life each moment – mind.

To live like a master we first need to notice that we hold within everything that we can use to design our future. We're meant to be a superhuman.

Need proof? Then prove it to yourself right away.

Imagine doing all that you do now only a century ago.

See all the posh vehicles around? Visualize the sophisticated gadgets world around is dying to own. And imagine the woozy speed at which life is changing around.

Tell me, "What would you have thought of them only a century ago?"

"Simply unbelievable!" Isn't it?

Quite similarly, the Bollywood hero overcoming mammoth challenges effortlessly might be only a magic on the screen. But this universe has bestowed us with a program in-built so that we too can evolve as a superhero!

And here's the secret to do so: It's a mind-thing.

It's all about connecting your awareness with the energy that forms the raw material for this universe. No, I am not speaking some metaphysical mumbo-jumbo. This is a reality we are blinding ourselves to.

In essence, we have all the stuff we ever needed to create everything we desire to be, do, and have. All we need to accept at this point is that we are born to live like a master!

With this in mind you just need to hit your restart button and launch yourself on this mission of authentic self leadership.

Excited to start anew?

Join me! Then the next crucial thing you will want to discover is...

...Why You Need To Take Charge?

Every time someone advised me to take charge I was angry. I would ask myself, "Aren't I already doing enough? Aren't I putting in my best efforts? Why then must I take responsibility for everything that happens to me?" The questions would puzzle me and leave me scratching my head.

With a little more self-reflection I discovered that we are made up of the same stuff that every object is made up of. We have something flowing through us which pervades the entire universe and connects us with the world around. Going a step deeper, we are also someone who is aware of all this. So we are something beyond what we experience and not what we see, touch, smell or feel. We are the one who goes through all of this and is aware of it at the same time. Isn't this something?

What if I told you are not just the material but are something beyond it? Because the truth is that you are the one who owns your body. The reality is that you have been experiencing life through your body. But you are something beyond it.

This knowledge is the first step to your inside-out life. Let it sink into you fully before you get to the next concept.

You and your body are usually mistaken as one. Believe me they are not. It's only that over time we start identifying ourselves with our bodies. This identification lies at the root of most miseries.

When did you last hear someone say, "My body is a little sick today?" Or "My body won't be able to come to office today?" This is because we have completely identified ourselves with our bodies. No one can deny it but the fact you will accept quickly is that you are the one who directs your body.

Remember, you take shelter in your body in the same manner that you take shelter in your house, dress, office etc. It's just about becoming more aware of who you are.

I know what you are thinking. No, I am not advocating any spiritual philosophy. Nor any religious school of thought, for that matter. It's absolutely practical.

Let me show you how.

Observe the people standing around someone who just passed away. You will notice something strange. You'll find that their perception of the person has completely changed. They start speaking and behaving as if they have just woken up to the fact that the person inside no more exists.

All of a sudden the person's name from Mr. /Ms XYZ has turned into 'the body'. In front of your eyes, the person's social identity seems to have evaporated.

Suddenly they start treating him as a body that has nobody inside. Something has vanished. What is 'that' something that just melted into thin air?

Simply put, the body just doesn't have the 'you' element inside.

Remember, you have always been with yourself. You are the one who has been observing your body grow until this day. Hence you are the observer, not the object. You have experienced it grow in front of your eyes. If you take a step forward and learn to detach yourself a little, you certainly can experience life at the next level.

Want to check it out for yourself? Here we go.

Picture yourself sitting in a closed chamber by yourself. Sit observing your thoughts for a while. Now take a step ahead and see yourself in the top corner of your room. And finally watch yourself from the top corner observing the 'you' sitting in the middle of the chamber... thinking.

I know you think you know it. No, you don't until you've done it. Take a few seconds and do it now. There's isn't any haste because I am with you till the end. Try the activity to get the hang of what I am saying. Don't let your mind trick you anymore.

Done? Do you realize what you just did?

You just disassociated yourself from your thinking-self. This is the awareness of being aware. It's a power that's available only to us – the humans! Now that you have done this, you are amongst the few special people who realize that they are different from other species and that there is something unique about them. Congratualtions.

We belong to a species which has a rare capability of detached observation. No other species has got such ability to detach two levels from themselves. Most people know about this but do not want to talk about it because this will ask them to explore something new.

John Flavell, the American developmental psychologist, labeled this rare higher-level cognition as 'meta-cognition'. Psychological jargon aside, studies show that be it meta-cognition or meta-reasoning or meta-perception, we can use them and create better lives for ourselves. The reason is that dissociated observation stimulates the higher brain functions which help you build a newer you!

Ask most experts and they will assent to the idea that you are fully equipped to create a new 'self-concept'. Your self-concept is the key to how you perceive the world around. More importantly, it is the key to how you perceive yourself.

The better your self-concept, the better is the result you experience. The clearer your self-concept, the clearer you become about what you intend to experience. That's exactly how you get ready to experience a richer and fuller life!

Only we as a human have this remarkable ability. Want to celebrate? Get yourself a cup of Coffee. I don't mind joining you.

Okay. Back?

Remember, we are a rare species designed to use all these remarkable faculties and, perhaps, for the same reason we tend to take them for granted.

Why else do you think we tend to ignore them? May be it is not because of the difficulty involved but because of how easy it is. And that is why most people settle for mediocre lives.

So now it's needless to prove anymore that we are neither our body, nor our mind. We are the one who own them.

Welcome to the deep sea!

How often have you seen your body falling sick and regain health? How often have you felt frustrated and watched peace restore?

The fact we ignore is that we are the ones who are going through the experience and are aware of what we experience. So we are not what we experience. We are beyond what's happening to us.

Doesn't that make clear that we are beyond what we have gathered from this planet? The reality is that our body is an accumulation from all that we have gathered from food. Our mind is an accumulation from all the impressions we gathered through our senses. But we are someone who has been experiencing health, sickness, well-being, mental disturbance and peace through your body and mind. So we are ones who own our body and mind.

If your question is who then is in charge of your life, the simple and straight answer is – YOU!

Now that you agree that you're beyond your body and mind, the question is: how do you experience your authentic being?

"By taking charge."

Get this - we have been gifted with two powerful tools - body and mind. We can use them to materialize your dream life. How? We just need to take charge and take leverage of our inner tools to experience our highest level of being.

FACT: We are already working like a magnet constantly exchanging energy with the universe. We are already creating all that we are going through. We are a magnet.

The most underrated truth behind all positive thinking philosophy is that you become what you think about most. Thinking is creating.

Observe the conversations among most of the 'impossible-thinking' groups. You will see the heights of pessimism. Their conversations revolve around the core idea of why something might 'not' work. What a colossal wastage of human potential. And what's more, they pump all their thought-power into failing themselves.

The central point behind the positive thinking theme is that we are innately able to think consciously. And that we attract what we think about most. All we need to realize is that we are at the helm of the affairs. All we need to do is get in tune with the source and connect with our authentic self.

But how do you do it?

Well, what do we do when we wish to watch our favorite program on a television channel? We tune the receiver of the television to the required frequency using our remote control. Exactly in the same manner we can also change the way we think. We choose the frequency of the desired thought and then tune into it. This is what you are going to explore further in the next chapters.

After all, by now you probably know that a lot of effort goes into designing and manufacturing even the latest TV in your living room. What I want you to know is that your journey becomes easy and effortless when you have the road map in your hands.

So take one step ahead and think...

... How You Can Plug into God's Hotline?

On a dark cloudy night, over a decade and a half ago, I found myself desperate for change in life. As if life had rejected me, I had almost given in to circumstances. I spent my days hoping against hope that I am going to see my happy days once again.

As a last attempt, I stood on the roof terrace and gazed intently towards the sky in utter desperation and heard myself shout in my head, "HELP."

I guess it's natural. If you are like me, you too do the same when you feel stuck in life. In a desperate attempt for one more chance at life, I too did this.

Even as I was desperate, hopeless, and crying for help, I woke up to a new reality. I felt as if someone invisible force wanted me to know that underlying principles of life are same for all.

I woke up to the fact that it is the same energy that pervades the whole universe. You name it God, Energy, Shakti or Chi - it doesn't matter what you call it. It is in interaction with 'that' source energy that we create everything in our life – physical or mental.

Toss this idea around for a second and allow your mind to absorb it fully because this is going to be the bedrock of all that you are going to explore further.

The new reality for me was that we are constantly exchanging energy with 'that' source and that it's a never ending process. It is in exchange of energy with 'that' source that we constantly create our life.

Bam! – I felt alive!

I knew it from within that this is exactly how we enter into an eternal partnership with the source. I call it a creative partnership.

Back to you: Are you still worried about your capacity to live your dream? Take it from me - you cannot give away something you don't have. You cannot create something with stuff you don't already have. Similarly, the source could not have made you with stuff it never possessed.

So this proves beyond any doubt that we are made of the same stuff that the source is made up of. To feel rejected, disappointed, and hopeless is only a sign of disconnection with the source within. To hit your restart button and become what you can, you just need to step into your higher self.

How? Exactly the same way you tune for your favorite show on your TV. All of it boils down to one point: It's all about making up with life. It's all about taking the reins back into your hands. It's all about exploring the art of authentic self leadership.

So what's the easiest way you can do it?

At this point let me introduce you to the awesome duo once again – mind and body. The only way you can do it easily is by disciplining these two powerful devices you are gifted with. To explore authentic self leadership and live a life inside-out is to work at your energy level first.

The question is: Where do you begin? Let's see.

Observe nature: We are naturally designed to grow and to ripen enough to drop down. Have you ever seen a fruit arguing with the tree, "Come on! How long are you going to hold me back?" I haven't. It just falls down naturally. Similarly, you grow from within. Rather, that's the only possible way it can happen.

Wait until you read the companion copy 'You.2 – A Crash Course In Authentic Self Leadership' where you will get simple ways reinvent yourself. Relax as I hand-hold you through the process.

Disciplining your inner tools is the first step because that's how you get aligned with the source at the energy level. Would it be an uphill attempt? Of course it's not going to be a cakewalk. Else why would you even bother to be here? But you are here because you have committed to give all it takes to create a fulfilled life for yourself.

At the same time you will find it much easier than your self-induced idleness, and even much easier when you know the system. The question is...

...Do You Have It In You?

"If you've come here to become a monk, do you have the 'will' enough to become one?" asked my spiritual guru Swami Ranganathananda when I met him in 1997 at Sri Ramakrishna Math, Hyderabad.

"Of course!" I shot from the hip.

Just fifteen days into monk's life, I caught myself thinking of ways to escape. I think it happened because I was not natural. He was natural. What I had in me was a mere wish. On the opposite, he was fully in tune with the source and that is because he was in tune with his purpose.

It took me years before I finally got in tune with my purpose which happened when I discovered that we can experience 'that' inner strength only when we have a clear purpose.

"Having a purpose in life plays a key role in keeping body and soul together for a long time," says Ram Seva Pathak – a 105 year old veteran Gandhian from Madhya Pradesh, India.

This only proves what Earn Nightingale spoke about in his 1957-audio 'strangest secret' which lay foundation to all the personal development movement. To illustrate his point, just imagine two ships - one without a captain or compass to help steer it, and the other with an expert to control.

What could be the fate of the two? It's not difficult to predict. Which one would you like to visualize yourself on?

> "'Circumstances do not make a man, they reveal him',
> -JAMES ALLEN"

To become what you are capable of is neither to renounce everything nor to indulge excessively because both are extremes.

According to Albert Bandura, the David Starr Jordan Professor Emeritus of Social Science Psychology at Stanford University, we are naturally built to grow despite the circumstances.

So, it is the timid that run away and it is the weak minded who yield to the circumstances. Self Leadership is for the courageous. If you are not courageous enough to do what it takes and are merely wishing change, you are wasting your time here. You had better wait for your next promotion or keep job-hopping expecting change, or the best of all buy yourself a lottery ticket.

Look here. This book is for the committed, courageous and the ones who really intend to connect with their call.

Of course, we certainly need courage to take charge. But don't forget that we already have everything it takes to do it.

Mahatma Gandhi was indiscriminately thrown out of the train at Pietermaritzburg despite having a first-class ticket. This was his first taste of racial discrimination. He could have interpreted it in any way of his choice. Like most others he could have reacted by showing anger. However he chose to choose his response.

Most of us live life in reaction to circumstances. What he demonstrated was a rare display of the power of personal choice. Like David confronting Goliath he chose to transform his anger into a dream of a free nation. He had it in him.

Now, that's courage!

You get to feel the same courage when you are clear about your dreams. Clarity precedes courage. While courage with clarity of purpose can fire-up your passion, courage without clarity on purpose is sheer foolishness. I did not have it in me when my guru asked me because I was not clear inside.

If you are determined to tap the real source of energy within, you need to get clear about your purpose.

Once you tap the ultimate source of power, you get to find the answer of your question, "What's...

...The Secret Ingredient of Super Heroes?

*"'Average performers resign themselves to mediocrity, thinking that the elite are somehow smarter, faster and cut from a different cloth. I call this The Myth of Genius. '
-ROBIN SHARMA "*

A simple question for you. It is a no-brainer, actually! What do all the iconic people like Mahatma Gandhi, Mother Teresa, Nelson Mandela, Martin Luther King, Franklin Roosevelt and Swami Vivekananda have in common?

See, it's easy right?

They all are gifted with special abilities which make them super leaders. They use their super powers or super abilities to influence us in a life-changing way.

Right? Let's look at it closely.

How true do you think is the concept of superhuman powers? Doubtless, there are a few who have some supernormal abilities. But the question is do you need such magical powers to live your dreams? No. You don't.

To become a super hero of your own life you don't need any super human powers. And sadly unlike in action movies, when life is in trouble, there is no superhero to call a savior.

Now go back to the list and add one more person to it - YOU!

Too good to be true, isn't it?

You heard me right enough - YOU.

The list now sounds something like this - Mahatma Gandhi, Mother Teresa, Nelson Mandela, Martin Luther King, Franklin Roosevelt, Swami Vivekananda and YOU!

What's common in all the people in the new list?

Remember, you are in the list, now.

So, what's unique that we all possess in common? Even after adding the last name in the list with you, me, or anyone else.

Here's your answer: It is authentic self leadership.

All iconic people might come from different corners of the world and they might have various factors differentiating one from the other. But they have one trait in common – authentic self leadership.

And their goals were in sync with it.

Every single goal of theirs was directed at materializing their authenticity. And that's the reason why you still feel the ripples they left behind.

Now ask yourself: What differentiates them from all those who delivered great products to the world and still became history soon. Nobody remembers them. Sad that despite all their efforts they ended up nonentities. They just disappeared from history.

There were thousands who made a little noise and then vanished without trace. The question is how they were different from the earlier ones.

Here's what I found: the latter ones could not leave a legacy because whatever they had achieved was not in sync with their higher self. As a consequence all that they created did not last long or didn't make enough impact.

Put simply, they did not have a 'WHY' behind their 'WHAT'.

By now you must be beginning to understand that what we have in us is the power to mold our personality, to shape our future, to create our destiny, and to determine who and what we are – a power greater than any other power!

At least once in our life, we must have envied a super successful person, haven't we? I too did for sure. How often have you whispered to yourself in secret, "I wish I had those talents", "I wish I had those skills?"

Imagine creating a super-successful life and leaving a meaningful legacy. You would enjoy it, wouldn't you? The question is, "Do all those great people who achieve BIG have special physical powers to do so?"

You will find it soon. And as you slip further into the book you will first learn...

...What Makes Them Great

> "'What the superior man seeks is in him; what the small man seeks
> is in others.'
> – Confucius"

Let me tell you about a lady. You must have seen her as a little lady of no imposing presence. She recognized within a desire to answer her call. And she at once acted on it.

She later went on to receive an award as big as the noble prize for her contributions - Mother Teresa.

Now answer this: What would you think of Mother Teresa's physical strength? In what way was Mother Teresa physically powerful beyond any normal human?

Now I want your unconscious mind to listen very carefully when I say, "What you have is the power to know who you are, what you can do, and how you can do it. It's this power which everyone has a share of, and it can make anyone a leader in their own way."

Briefly, it is the power of authenticity.

So if you desire to LIVE BIG you need to THINK INWARDS and make the best use of the power within.

And if you've seen yourself as an ordinary being so far then then you need to ask...

... How You Can Reverse Your Perception?

We have got so tuned to outside that we have almost switched off to our inner being. We choose to make our lives so busy that we eliminate the slightest opportunity of peeping within? We are drowing in so much of outside that the inner side has become irrelevant.

Go back to your childhood. Didn't you resent it when your parents compared your results with those of your friend's? Haven't you secretly desired to become like someone else at least once?

Competition, huh?

It's everywhere. Each time your parents compared you with someone, they planted something in you - a way of looking at yourself from the outside perspective. In fact, for the first year and a half you didn't have an identity of your own. You were one with your mother. Once you began absorbing impressions from outside, you even got your perceptions downloaded into you. Most of what you think as yours today is what others told or thought or believed about you.

What if you had the power to reverse your perceptions? What if you could undo all that was impressed upon you by the outside world? What if you could announce yourself a success, when the world outside called you a failure?

Refreshing?! Curious when?

The instant you learn how to tap the power of your 'thoughts'.

Yes, it's that powerful!

First, if the world says you 'are not' and 'cannot', I want you to scream in your head in return, 'I AM', and therefore 'I CAN'.

So begin by changing your inside to see change in your outside. And take your first step forward in answering the question...

...What's Your Dream?

"'It is not logic or facts but our hopes and dreams, our hearts and our guts, that drive us to try new things'
-SIMON SINEK"

'Dream Life' --- the words remind me of the Indian romantic number 'Dream Girl'.

A super-hit love song from the Bollywood movie of 1980s. It goes like this... "Dream girl... Kisi shayar ki gazal, Dream Girl... Koi jheel ka kamal...dream girl."

If you've heard the song, you'll agree that the words softly nudge us into a fantasy world. And many a time, the fantasy trip screeches to a halt with the words – "Come on! Stop day dreaming; be realistic" or with "Oh, but it's only a dream."

Millions of dreams come to such a grinding halt when we foolishly crush them to death by not acknowledging them. They actually could be the most coveted 'dream lives' for most of us.

Now the dark side is that each time a dream gets crushed, we find against the backdrop the most dreadful human-coined words - "STOP DREAMING—BE REALISTIC."

Everything realistic and practical is a result of hard work and has nothing to do with anyone's dream. Isn't this what we are trained to believe? Do you know a time when you too believed the same? Do you see the impact these words create in our personal and professional lives? This is the belief which puts our life on the never-ending treadmill of 'existence-mindset'. (You'll learn more about this mindset in 'You.2 – A Crash Course In Authentic Self Leadership')

The challenge is how you can unshackle yourself from such an arresting influence of this limiting belief. There is only one way you can do it – by putting them in right perspective.

Let's me show you how.

Dreaming wouldn't have been a part of our evolution if it hadn't been of any use. Do you see the point? If dreaming hadn't been a part of our evolution, we could never have made all discoveries. Mostly we take all our discoveries for granted. But the question is how did they turn REAL?

Isn't it a fact that someone first dreamed of electricity for lights, fans and air-conditioning machines and only then worked to explore ways to build them? Think.

As far as I know, that's the only way creation happens.

Ask yourself: In this day and age, can we do away with them, for a second?

I doubt it.

Didn't someone dream of flying in the air before we discovered how to fly? Can you imagine life without thousands of sophisticated flights taking off from runways every second?

In a word, NO.

Don't you think someone must have dreamed of seamless connectivity? As a result we gained this instant access to people on the other side of the globe at a click of mouse.

Remember: We are living in a completely different world now. What's more, it might just be the beginning of the new beginning.

FACT: All life is physical creation of what you hold in your mind. And this is the essence of Earl Nightingale's 'The Strangest Secret'.

Sit back and read it over and over again.

If you stop reading further and take away this one point, and act on it, you will make your life wonderful.

It's explosive. Never underestimate the power of your dream. Instead, learn quickly how to tap this free resource available. All of us have equal access to world's resources undoubtedly. But before you can live your dream you need to cherish the dream in your heart long enough for it to take physical shape.

Eager to kick-start your life of achievements? Looking for the best time to begin something new? It's NOW!

Just name your dream and set the process of creation in motion!

Still have questions in mind? Excellent. That's the sign of an authentic self-leader in the making.

Read on if you are asking yourself...

...Why Dream?

I once frantically woke up in the middle of the night, jolted out of the blue by a nightmare and feeling totally exhausted. I found myself trembling with fear as the slight shake in my hands was still noticeable.

It was as if I had just chickened out of a reality show where participants are exposed to life-threatening creatures - totally nervous. I could even feel the throb in my head painfully.

In a weak attempt to comfort myself I said aloud, "It was a bad dream". Well, the reality was it was bad enough to keep me awake the whole night. I tried in vain to relax while and at the same time unconsciously trying to mentally recreate the experience.

I still wonder why on the earth was I doing that.

Do you remember the last time you tried to connect the missing links of your dreams? I believe most of us do this once we wake up after a dream, don't we?

But I was not going to leave it at that because I preferred to go deeper to understand the effect of the experience on me. I had always believed that this is the only way we could discover life's truths.

I began sequencing what I had been through. Here's how I was connecting the dots: I saw something in my dream... experienced some emotions... and felt they were real. For a while I was out of touch with the reality and felt threatened... wanted to be safe... wanted to be alive... and snapped myself out of sleep... and was confused for the next few seconds. Finally, I took time to come to terms with reality. Thus I successfully recreated the sequence in my mind.

But there was something more distinct that I discovered. I had sweat on my forehead. REAL. Because I could touch it. I could see my hands shaking. I could feel my head throbbing hard, and I was nervous all-over. My nervous system was going through the experience in real.

Over the next few hours I kept brooding over all that and finally, after what I realized, I felt as if I have cracked a significant code - Dreams are real!

I realized that a dream in an unconscious state of mind had deep psychosomatic effects. The question firing the neurons in my head was, "Can I harness the same power and consciously create a dream?"

"Yes, I CAN", I heard a voice from within.

By now if you know what I am trying to bring home, I don't have to convince you anymore.

Here are three truths you can anchor in your mind forever: To dream is to create, to dream is to gain access to the all-powerful energy, and to dream is to have an unflinching faith in the creative power of the universal energy.

Ask anyone who has re-created himself, and you will get a super-simple advice, "Have a dream!"

Because to dream is to crack the mysteries of future as it simply allows you to get a quick glimpse of what's in store for you. In other words, dreams show you what you choose to experience in future.

The sooner you get willing to go ahead, the quicker you'll able to harness the power of your free-will. So dreaming is to co-create your future and architect the future time.

Okay. Now that you've got the word 'dreaming' in right perspective, let's begin to examine...

...*What is Being REALISTIC?*

This is just between you and me. Each time someone said, "Be realistic," I was angry. I felt it a freely available way to confine ourselves. The two words sounded as the key to a self-defeating world.

"How to instantly get free from this self-delusion?" turned a riddle for me. If you too are thinking the same, then ask yourself, "Am I taking the two words 'Be Realistic' for being pessimistic?"

The point is, what do you understand these words as?

What's your definition of being realistic?

What do 'be realistic' sound like to you? Do they sound like 'Why something won't be possible' or 'Why we can't do something' or 'Why we can't earn the money we wish for' or 'Why we can't buy something that we want to' or 'Why we can't... can't... can't... and can't? To put it simply, do they invoke thoughts of limitations?

If this is how they sound to you, then here's something valuable you might want to consider. I have heard the words over a million times, and I believed them so deeply until I suddenly realized something life-changing. That all those who said these words had a strange quality in them. For some peculiar reason they had their right foot pressed on the brakes of their vehicle and were pushing hard 'NOT' to take their inspired leap.

However rude it might seem, the truth is they somehow ensured they were stuck in mediocrity. Think.

The bitter truth of life is that the average is addictive.

"Take care", they told themselves. They had been playing safe for very long. The tragedy is they had done it so long that they forgot to 'take charge'. They were addicted to average and failed to explore the authentic self-leader within.

They had already developed a lens with a limited view and could see only so far. Now if you are trying to see through their limited-view lens, remember, "Their reality need not be yours."

Stop spending years searching for answers outside. In fact, you can upgrade your limited-edition self to a new expanded-self once you understand that the words and the thought of 'take care' emerge from the state of mind of 'lack' and 'insecurity'.

Here's the secret to anybody's success: Each one of us has the right and free will to choose the view as well as the device to view life!

At this point I want to make you a promise.

In the next few pages, I am going to share every bit of insider information I have gathered so far from my unrelenting search for truth. It could save you years. Imagine.

In my long journey of personal transformation, I found that to 'be practical' is to think possibility. It was an eye-opener for me that 'being realistic' is to explore life with an unflinching faith in the scope for possibility and that you can really do what you want to.

I don't want you to foolishly believe this and think that just about anything you wish to do is possible. But your capacity to respond to everything that happens is truly limitless. And the truth is that your limits are farther than you've accepted them to be. At least ten times. See the point? And trust me that's huge!

To 'be realistic' is to seek all the means and ways to get ignited from inside and make your dream come true.

Here's the bottom line: to 'be realistic' is not to think about why something cannot be done. Rather, it's only and only to think why something can be done.

Will Smith says it better, "I know who I AM. I know what my belief is. I am willing to die for it. Period."

Isn't this is the true meaning of being realistic! Sounds good?

> " "Being realistic is the most commonly travelled road to
> mediocrity." – Will Smith "

So finally you have put 'Dreaming' and being 'realistic' in right perspective.

Ready to jet off to your dream life?

Say yes to life?

That's g-r-e-a-t! Let's start by identifying...

...What's unique in the successful?

As your mind begins to answer the question above, consider one more - What is the unique trait common to all the legendary names here – Mahatma Gandhi, Mother Teresa, Nelson Mandela, Martin Luther King, Franklin Roosevelt and Swami Vivekananda? To stress again, it plays a key role behind the success of millions.

What's the trait which makes them live a life of personal choice? What's the single most important thing that differentiates them from those who fail to get what they want?

Scratching your head? Look closely into their stories.

Here's what differentiates them: They 'took charge!'

They took charge of their fates. They decided to redesign their destinies. They took personal responsibility to carve a new self. Be it in personal life or career - it's easily understood their success was not by some freak of fate. In fact, there is no such thing as a free lunch.

> *"Peak performance begins with your taking complete responsibility*
> *for your life and everything that happens to you.'*
> *BRIAN TRACY*

The secret behind their success was their all-consuming dream. The first thing they convinced themselves of was, "Boy, get ready to stretch your safe zones!"

This is how authentic self-leaders ignite the desire within and turn their dream a reality. What's more, they put it right at the top of their list of priorities.

In short: They have an all-consuming idea, they give the idea their life, and do what it takes. It's worth reading a hundred times.

"Man is a goal striving mechanism", said Maxwell Maltz. The key is to learn to focus your energy exactly on what you want to create. From what I gather, you always chase a goal at any point in time. Whether you choose it, or accept it from external environment, it's inevitable that you are chasing a goal.

Take it from me, you are designed that way. You are bound to chase a goal every second you breathe. If your goal is one absorbed from outside, it could be anything ranging from gossiping, to making an unnecessary call, to going to a movie just to kill time, to smoking, to listening to entertaining songs and so on.

On the opposite, if it's inspired from within, it could be anything like: to become a public speaker, to read at least one good book every month, to attend a seminar, to meditate every day, to join a health or fitness club and so on and so forth which are focused on personal evolution or to help you live a better story.

> *"There is immense spiritual power and strength within an*
> *individual when faced with the choice to continue living as a victim*

of a tragic accident or to seize the opportunity of 'life'
– SAMUEL 'SAM' CAWTHORN "

Let's get to the point. If you are asking me, "What differentiates the successful from the mediocre", Here's your answer, "They have a compelling dream, a burning desire, and trust in their capacity to turn it real." This is what self efficacy is all about.

They first focus on the 'why' part of the dream and then get to the 'how' part because they somehow put faith in the creative force of this universe. They choose the meaning they wish to create, get restless to find the larger purpose behind their dreams, and create value for themselves and everyone around. They do it by connecting with their authentic self within.

The question is what is the larger purpose behind your dream? The answer would give you your 'why'. Remember, the answer holds the secret for you to hang on a little longer.

Put another way, knowing the 'why' behind your goals makes you clearer, committed, and courageous. And that's when you begin to learn...

...How to Unlock Success?

Success happens at three levels. It is a 'heart' thing first, a 'mind' thing next and a 'physical' last. We are educated to believe it the opposite way.

People who live a legendary life have a 'purpose' in their heart, 'goal' in their mind and then apply themselves to turn it real!

All in all, the purpose of your life is the larger cause you live for. It is an anchor you align your goals to. Every choice you make then gets in tune with your purpose. At the same time it's like a compass you can follow to walk across the multitude of choices. In effect, it's the light house that helps you make sound decisions and direct you to your dream!

With this in mind they re-script their story by restructuring their self-system. They first choose a compelling dream and then develop personal beliefs which help them sync with their call.

Naturally, the journey of your success begins when you take full responsibility. The fact you are so focused until here is the unquestionable proof that you have decided to become an authentic self-leader, and also that you are willing to explore the power in your hands.

The question is: What happens when you take charge?

Here's what happens: The instant you take charge, you choose to build a life-philosophy to experience life in a certain way. And once you choose a life-philosophy, everything you need begins to oscillate towards it as if by magic because your philosophy becomes your model of reality.

The people you need, the books you need, the advisors you need, the ideas you need, and the resources you need - everything seems to fall into place. EVERYTHING.

This is exactly when you get a free hand at designing your future. The moment you choose your 'WHY', you spark your inner drive and get a reason to grab your dream long enough to turn it real because your why becomes the glue holding your life together.

For long we have been told that only 3% of those who begin to achieve a goal stick to it for long enough. At least for the argument sake, why are the majority unable to do so? What must be the reason?

Here's my take on it: The cause of their lack of persistence doesn't lie in the goal. It's hidden in the life-philosophy beneath it. It wasn't strong enough to fire their passion.

With a weak philosophy of life one can never go that extra mile because when setbacks set in, life falls apart, and the spirit is broken; it's your personal life-philosophy that keeps the hope in you alive. It rekindles your passion, guides you to do the things you are meant for, and helps you keep on!

Back to you: If you have decided to rebuild yourself, take your first step forward by choosing a 'major purpose' now. Once you have a clear purpose, your dreams now become the 'by-products' of your 'major purpose'. That's exactly how you begin championing the cause of life.

You are now free to grow!

Now that you know how crucial a life-philosophy and a purpose is to your life, take your next step and choose your dream, direct all your energy on it, and set goals to achieve it.

Hey! I am more than excited to be with you on this adventurous journey of personal reinvention. Wait until you complete the first part 'The Authentic Self Leadership Mindset' and get to the companion copy of this book 'You.2 – A Crash Course In Authentic Self Leadership' to get the step-by-step system to do it.

To sum up the key points:

- You will find it easier to empower yourself from within once you choose to create a life of your own choice.
- You will be fired-up once you take personal responsibility to do everything.
- You can become a superhero the instant you realize that real power lies in your capacity to choose.

And if you're waiting for the time to begin, and probably asking when's...

... The Best Time To Launch Yourself?

Success seekers never put off personal change. Any expert will agree that all successful people act on life-changing actions with an extreme sense of urgency. They never put off personal transformation. They resolve to do it now.

In fact, mentally, they do things yesterday.

This is how the successful think and act. They first dream something BIG that makes no sense to the 97% people around and then throw their 100% to do what it takes.

NO EXCUSES.

How do they do it?

Get this - they 'take charge' in the moment!

They take full responsibility for all that is going to happen in their lives and live a conscious life. And then you hear people say, "Oh, he must be gifted", "Nope, not everyone can do it". "Not me" and so on and so forth.

The truth is they might not necessarily be gifted. Far from it, they choose to take full responsibility of their life. Even for the setbacks. They choose to keep an open mind and become available to the gifts the universe.

You see the same change in your life once you take charge. And then understand from experience that universe reveals itself to everyone unconditionally, but only when you know how to knock and give it the necessary blow. This is how you master the art of authentic self leadership.

Need more proof?

The simple truth that you have chosen this book proves you are a rare thinking person. And the very point you are still with me only proves you already are a master stuff.

Imagine a companion alongside while you reinvent yourself. Hit Your Restart Button is going to be one for you. You have no idea how millions still await inspiration. What if you were that inspiration to all who intend to live a life of self-reliance, self-efficacy, and natural self-confidence? Imagine.

Remember, you always get the best stuff wrapped up in challenges. You might have already faced many and today life has thrown one more at you - a challenge to empower yourself, to re-script your destiny, and to create your own future.

"Are you ready to launch yourself?"

"Yes?"

"How can you do it right away?"

"Identify the real source of power. As we come towards the end of the beginning, you probably absorb that all of this starts at one point – YOU!"

If you are asking, "When?"

"Only when you take up the reins!"

In the next chapter I am going to reveal the barricades we have erected on our own path to realization. It's crucial we deal with them before we go deeper. And we will also find how life rewards us once we begin to acknowledge the power within.

Here's the bottom line: This certainly is a challenge but a zero-risk one. I know what you are looking for – the catch right?

Yes, there is one. You risk losing your present self. You risk losing your ego, your past, and your limited identity that you've spent years building.

But isn't this what you have come here for?

Decide now.

Sounds tempting?

Then join me now on this adventurous journey inwards, get your creative juices flowing, spread your wings, aaand... get ready for take off!

CHAPTER THREE

SHOOT THE SEVEN-HEADED MONSTER

"You cannot be wimpy out there on the dream-seeking trail. Dare to break through barriers, to find your own path."
-Les Brown

CONFESSION: BACK IN THE DAYS when I first got inspired from some of the great leaders I used to think they were lucky. Years later a good friend of mine once told me, "It's not luck. It's how they faced and handled their barriers that transformed them."

Can you look in the eye of your fear and confirm you are there to win? If your answer is a YES, then the odds are very much in your favor.

Observe how the authentic self-leaders respond to barriers. They never blindfold themselves to the obstacles. In fact, at the sight of a slightest obstacle they say, "Here's one more opportunity?"

Wish to explore yourself as a free spirit? Then realize that the human spirit is naturally gifted to grow. Expansion is the mantra and is the only way you can become who you are designed to be.

How often have you thought of upgrading your 'self'?

Wondering how you can?

You don't realize it yet but it's the best thing you can do to yourself. However, it can be self-defeating if you hope to do it without confronting the usual dosage of barriers.

Here's the seven-headed monster you must conquer before you unlock your high-impact version. The leader is the...

1. Fear of failure

""The greatest barrier to success is the fear of failure"
- SVEN GORAN ERIKSSON"

Studies prove that as a child we are born with only two fears - fear of loud noises and fear of falling. All other fears are what we gathered from environment.

How often have you thought of dedicating yourself to projects which never saw the first ray of sunshine? You will be shocked if you list all of them.

If you are looking for the most common reason for this streak of failures, here's the devil - Fear of Failure.

It's found to be the prime reason why most people never begin. We are raised to be afraid of failure. We are conditioned to avert failure even when we are designed to grow. "Fear isn't only a guide to keep us safe; it's also a manipulative emotion that can trick us into living a boring life," says Donald Miller in his New York Times Bestseller A Millions Miles In A Thousand Years.

Observe a toddler. Watch it making its first attempts to stand straight up and walk right. Remember when you tried your first unsteady step before you began to toddle about? It was all fine until we lost balance, fell repeatedly, and accepted it as natural. Everyone around thought, "It's okay. It's natural."

No one said, "Hey, don't get up. You will fall down. You had better crawled by your whole life." Everybody around cheered us to make one more attempt.

Suddenly, something went wrong. As we grew older, we heard a voice from somewhere, "BE SAFE." People started projecting their fears upon us. "You had better be safe than fail", the voices around began imposing. Mostly you heard them from people with authority in your life – family. That is why the idea got easily planted in your subconscious. The tragedy is that we got programmed to fear failure even before we learnt how to make our choices. See the missing link?

This is exactly why; it remains the leader of all barriers. If you've just said, "I am decided to make life exciting come what may, then learn how to channel your fears in the right direction.

Look on the bright side. Wonder how?

Keep reading further. The next on the list of barriers is...

2. Seeking Validation

Ask obese people and mostly you will discover something common. It's their emotional turmoil that gradually led to a weight problem. In most cases, their personal grief and emotional suppression is beneath their approval seeking attitude.

A close friend of mine once admitted, "I needed everyone to like me, because I didn't like myself much. I ended up in undignified relationships with guys who'd tell me how mean I was, and I'd nod in agreement, "Oh thank you, you're so right."

Why? Because she had no sense she deserved something better. This is why she admits she gained so much weight later on. Lack of self-love was the culprit. Seeking validation and approval was her way of cushioning herself against the world's disapproval.

Let's go a little deeper. Seeking approval is like expecting a 'yes' for everything you do. You turn a dependent eager to admit, "I will do this task when most people approve it."

Well, it's not your fault at all because this is how we are conditioned to live. As a child you had to seek permission for anything you wanted to do? The questions would range from "What are you doing?" to "What are you thinking?" Oh come on - you can't even think in secret? But that built a pattern as you grew older and you turned a slave to the pattern.

That's how you got used to expecting a 'yes' for everything you did. The world outside became your locus of control. While you allowed yourself full reins, the approval seeking behavior subconsciously started convincing you otherwise.

It programmed you to seek validation for every choice you made. What should I study... what should I wear... what suits me... where shall I go... who should I choose as my partner... and on and on and on. You kept seeking approval even on trivialities.

I hear you asking, "How can I stop seeking validation and become naturally confident?"

"By retraining your mind to see that each one of us is a unique unit of life seeking personal growth."

Remember we all are particles of the same energy but at the same time, we are unique in our purpose.

Although the fundamental purpose of life is growth, our unique purpose is for us to dig and explore. The fact is that the fundamental purpose common to all is growth and that we are designed to grow and expand. To realize this is our first step to get tuned to the creative life force.

If you've cursed your environment at some point, let me tell you, the environment around is meant only to be instrumental in your exploration.

Seth Godin, international bestselling author, says he stopped reading online reviews of his books years ago, and adds that nothing bad has happened to him by reading zero. He says, "It doesn't make my work better for me to hear anonymous people tell me I don't know what I am doing. But we seek it out."

Martin Seligman in his book Flourish establishes how growth is a personal choice. To seek approval is like wanting somebody to say, "You are worth living." And only then you breathe on your own. In such behavior you always tend to react. You don't act; you only react. And you always want the outside world to approve your reality.

To increase your awareness about your behavior, ask yourself:

- Am I an approval seeker?
- Do I excessively rely on others' opinions?
- How is this preventing me from realizing my goals?

Once you begin to know it from inside, you come closer to overcoming another big barrier. It's the...

3. Fear of Rejection

Ages ago we began to live in groups. It's common understanding that we did it for survival. The communities started evolving at physical and emotional levels because essentially they were meant to nurture, nourish, and help us grow socially.

With the evolution of this system of living in groups, we developed a pattern - a pattern of living in circles. We still continue to live in circles and we are part of many circles ranging from family to organizational and social circles.

However, the crucial thing we need to understand is that the system we developed for our societal evolution has become the very reason stilting our growth.

Why? Because we started clinging to our circles. The circles were meant to give us an environment conducive to growth but they gradually proved detrimental to our expression in some unknown way?

How? I have the reason. We are afraid to look inwards, and that's why we keep looking outwards for answers. We fear that the circle we belong to would become cynical of us. We don't dare speak openly about our ideas. We fear losing our social affiliation. We forget that it's not about the circles but about how we treat them.

As clock ticks away, we get firmly rooted in this insecurity. We feed the fear that the groups would abandon us. Eventually this develops as a habit of living 'outside-in'. The external world becomes more dominating than your inner world – your authentic 'self'. People outside become the locus of control and their opinions begin to matter most.

An in-depth look will prove that our search for belongingness if misunderstood turns another reason that blocks us from expressing ourselves fully. We seem to have etched it deep in our minds that we are nothing until we belong to somebody so much so that we have turned our backs on the 'self'.

I am surprised how most people look for somebody to say, "You are mine." We accept that we 'are' something only when somebody says we belong to them. Else we 'are not'?! This is how we get stuck in the state of lack.

Want to prove it to yourself?

How often do you revisit your Facebook account only to check the number of likes your post attracted?

Got it? That's craving for approval from outside. This prevents you from looking inwards and this stops you from taking personal responsibility. You don't take it for the fear that it may distance you from those who give you the sense of belongingness. That's exactly why most people just can't resist sharing every single detail of their daily life on social media.

Know someone who does it?

Remember, seeking validation makes you weaker and curtails your sense of freedom and autonomy.

Authentic self leadership is all about freedom and autonomy.

Here's one more reason why people avoid responsibility - our search for personal identity from the groups. Instead of identifying our real nature, we seek it from the groups we belong to.

Although I don't discourage affiliation to groups it's high time we remembered that our sense of identity is inbuilt. We are born with talents unique to us. We are built and naturally designed to accomplish our purpose.

In fact, it's our purpose that gives us our true identity. The groups are meant only to facilitate the process and be the mirror to our 'self'. They are not for us to draw our identities from. It's true that you're the average of the five people you constantly hang out with but it's your purpose that gives you the true identity.

You do not become something just because you belong to a certain group. You have your identity inbuilt! You have skills and talents to extend your services through the groups.

The question is: Where then is the root of this fear?

The roots lie in expecting permanency in relationships.

"Will you love me forever?"

"Will you be mine forever?"

Sounds familiar?

This very expectation of permanency distances us from life in the present moment and you start finding solace in future. Once you start doing it, you begin to ignore the moment in hand. And all these thoughts of fear can only bring true the circumstances we fear.

So when does this fear go?

Only when you allow yourself to believe that there is nothing permanent. Nothing but change.

You've probably heard it that the only constant is change. Everything is in a process of transformation. You do not have to stall your growth for the fear of losing people. Remember they too have been gifted the right to choose their own growth.

Last but not least, whether you choose it or not, life will certainly nudge you into challenges fostering growth. None will be left out. You had better use your right to choose, thrust yourself towards your purpose, and do it before the universe thrusts upon you challenges. Especially those which you might never want to appreciate. Think.

While you get ready to free yourself instantly, one stealthy culprit you must be on the lookout for is...

4. Expecting 100% Clarity

Here's another reason which poses a threat to your journey of authentic self leadership. It is purely mental - 'expecting 100% clarity about your future'.

Surprisingly, the only solution to the problem is hidden within the expectation. It starts with clarity about the concept of 'future'. What you must know is that your perception about future decides your approach towards the future.

Read it twice before you proceed further.

To expect complete clarity about future is a passive approach to life. I agree that desire and expectation are powerful states of mind. And they are highly essential for personal reinvention but they remain to be passive states only. They cannot bring results just by themselves.

"Let me first get complete clarity on future and only then will I take action." If this is what you say to yourself, you must know it is you who creates your future.

How? By choosing a few from all the probabilities you have in the present moment. Remember, the probabilities are infinite!

In essence, your future is an ever unfolding mystery. It is an extension of your mind. Your mind stretched in time and space is your future. You in the future are nothing but a projection of the image of yourself that you behold in your mind at the present moment.

You need to have clarity on first: your mind doesn't function like a camera; it functions like a projector.

Hence, what you think you 'are' now is what moulds into your future. What you think in the present moment develops itself into circumstances in your future time. Your state of mind in the present moment is what creates your experience in the future. Who you think you 'are' now is who you 'are' going to be in the future also because this is what you are projecting onto the canvas of consciousness.

Keep in mind that your future is in the making every moment you hold a thought about yourself in the 'now'. It's is a game of 'probabilities'. Your friend and foe in choosing the right probability is 'emotion'.

Yes, emotional instability can blind you to the right decision as your impulse takes over your conscious thinking. At the same time expecting 100% clarity about future is a passive approach to life. You do not actively contribute your share in this approach. You only react; not create. What a colossal wastage of creative energy! And what if we consider this at a national scale? And then on an international scale?

Want to prevent this extreme wastage?

Then download into yourself that the absence of 100% clarity is one of our primal needs to help us explore life and grow naturally. The path to clarity is through confusion. There is nothing technically wrong in expecting 100% clarity and working towards clarity, but expecting it without a prior dosage of confusion is an illusion.

Now here's what makes it more significant: It is a real need because it is closely linked with your capacity - the capacity to choose your response. What you need to absorb is that you have an inbuilt 'free will'. And that's exactly why you cannot have a rigid and fixed plan of future.

In other words, there can never be a fixed future in a universe made of unlimited probabilities. Do you get it? Had it been a fixed affair, you would never have been gifted with free-will - the capacity to choose. It's a boon!

This capacity to choose always is in the present moment. You can make your choices only in the present. Hence you are creating your future 'now'. You have the right and the capacity to choose your future. You can do it only by employing your 'free will'.

And the good news is that it's absolutely free!

Let me give you a concrete example: Have you ever noticed the thrill we feel while watching a movie for the first time? Did you notice the second time it goes down by a little? And this continues until it fades away.

You probably know why this happens – familiarity breeds contempt. This happens because we are pre-informed of what is going to unfold. Your brain finds it boring because there's no challenge. The secret is out. The same happens when you get 100% clarity of what future holds in store for you.

This brings us to another powerful concept that the absence of clarity about future leaves us an unlimited domain of choices in the present moment. It's freedom!

Authentic self leadership is all about being an explorer at heart and seeking freedom from within. What's more, it offers you a great opportunity to co-create your own destiny.

Much as this book calls for a step of change, it really helps you turn this barrier into your aide for success. What you just need to do is hit your restart button and you will see yourself hitting your strides.

A word of caution: The one powerful enemy which you must conquer to go ahead undeterred is...

5. Indulging In Blame Game

99 percent of people you meet every day will find rationale in blaming the circumstances, colleagues, friends, education, family, finances, or something external for their adversity. Most people hold something outside responsible for their suffering.

They deny personal responsibility and play the 'poor me' role seeking sympathy. Some of their words would be like...

'If only I had more money'

'If only I had better resources'

'If only I had gone to a better college'

'If only I had a better laptop...mobile...books'

'If only I had better opportunities'

'If only I had a better boss'

'If only I had ....'

Sounds familiar?

Let's try to understand the underlying mechanism.

Remember, it's futile to locate the cause outside. I know you're asking why. Here's why: the world outside only represents something going on inside. Blaming something outside gives us an excuse from the outcome - a chance to repeat the mistake and escape the responsibility for the consequences.

Point to think?

Another reason hidden beneath the 'blame game' is a desire for validation. It indicates a low self-esteem or a distorted perception of gaining prominence through sympathy. It has its source in identity crisis.

"It's the system", we seem to have grown a fixation with these words. Want to know what this does to you?

It only installs in us a victim-mindset.

This very externally driven perception of life becomes the cause for inner suffering. You can't imagine what harm it does to you through your own self defeating inner-talk, and by indulging in accepting a poor self image.

Here's what happens the instant you shift the blame outwards: you not only fix blame but also give away the responsibility of your success to that external element.

It's worth reading a zillion times.

Now stop and see yourself at the top of a horse. You wish to enjoy a thrilling ride but find that the horse is being controlled by someone else.

How do you feel?

Powerless? Helpless?

Exactly in the same way, we make ourselves powerless when we fix the blame on something outside. We become passive and give away the reins of your life to some unknown external factors and turn ourselves drones.

Suddenly everything in our life is being controlled by something outside. That's exactly how the 'blame game' becomes a big roadblock on our journey of authentic self leadership.

Above all, as long as we don't take full responsibility to change our life, we will be constantly pricked by an invisible enemy inside. And here's the enemy within for you to conquer first. It's...

6. Guilt

What is guilt? It is an affective state of mind in which you experience an inner conflict. We experience a negative feeling at having done something we know we shouldn't have. Or haven't done something we should have. It gives rise to a feeling called 'guilt'.

You can compare this state of mind with a marshy land. Neither it goes away easily, nor does it allow you to move forward. A tricky state of mind.

Sigmund Freud explained this as the result of struggle between ego and superego.

'I should not have used such language'

'I should have used my time properly'

'I should not have ....'

Heard before?

Let's dive in.

To get stuck in this state is a conscious choice. It's our mind's silly attempt to stretch the past into the present. It's like wanting to continue living in the past. We can also take it as an impractical attempt to correct the past in the past.

Why? The reason for this lies in our unpreparedness to accept the present circumstances unconditionally. It hides within a subliminal escapist attempt from taking responsibility for the present.

We choose NOT to act in the present moment and we do not employ our right to choose our response. And in doing so, we try to evade the responsibility for the consequences.

A stealthy culprit, huh?

Guilt is cyclic in nature. We spend time thinking about the reasons we couldn't be, do or have something. As if by some hidden law, the more we indulge in such thoughts the more we attract the same.

It's a crunching emotion which makes us give way to inertia and inaction. Gradually, we start rejoicing in our helpless past and co-create a victim present while unknowingly designing a battered future.

FACE IT: Like most other self defeating emotions, guilt also is a personal choice.

How can you overcome it?

The single best way is to 'take charge'. Become proactive. Take full responsibility for your action as well as the consequences. The bonus - it also cures two of its byproducts - inaction and inertia.

Here's the bottom line: Once you've decided to change your life by becoming an authentic self-leader, you must enhance your self-image too. You can't run a film of poor quality within and expect a good projection on the screen.

You can do it by consciously choosing powerful responses to circumstances you come across. And once you start enhancing your self-image, you begin to reclaim complete supremacy on this moment – your moment of empowerment!

CAUTION: You will always have one barrier very close to you each time you intend to move forward. It's the...

7. Fear of Change

The most damaging of all fears is the fear of change.

It originates in the habit of accepting the status quo as a permanent phenomenon. We don't want to lose something because we have grown comfortable with it. We just won't leave it, even if it hurts. It's like we love a food item and want the same food at your table for every meal.

Even if it stinks. Ugh!

We slowly get used to it and then build the binding chain around preventing us from accepting change. As simple as that.

What do you think is the cause?

It's our distrust in the unknown.

We don't put trust in the mystery element of life. Fear of change is rooted in the fear of exploring the unknown. It's rooted in our fear of trekking the uncharted territories.

We naturally resist change. How often have you found it hard to switch off your television? Bill Hicks, the top American standup comedian said, "Watching television is like taking black spray paint to your third eye?" Mind naturally gets attached to what it experiences for certain duration. It resists moving on. How often have you caught yourself helplessly glued to your television knowing you have other important things to do? It's resistance at work. Got the reason now?

And that's perhaps the same reason why most people find it difficult to let go of their mobile phones before retiring to bed.

Here's the truth: It's an undeniable fact that the very evolution of life depends on the exploration of the unknown. Nothing would have ever been discovered without this adventurous ingredient.

The secret of successful people mostly is their spirit of adventure. Their appetite for the unknown is THE SECRET to

their greatness. Their passion to dig into the mystery holds the technique. And that's the best possible way to embrace life.

Excited for the trip within?

Here's the first step inwards:

Fill the authentic self leadership pledge on the next page and commit to the process. By doing this you commit to creating a newer YOU!

Ready?

Turn the page...

My Authentic Self Leadership Pledge

I, _____, (Your first name) understand that my dreams will come true only when I act on them.

I am willing to explore the authentic self-leader within.

I understand that the consequences are always proportionate to the intensity of my desire and integrity.

I pledge to give my best shot at it as I understand that life is too short to be wasted on cheap distractions.

I know that the journey is going to be rough. I also know that I am going to be tough.

I know it's going to be a long journey and that I am going to have great fun throughout.

I also choose to share my knowledge with everyone willing to take charge and become authentic self-leaders.

I take full responsibility for my past, present and the future that I am going to create henceforth.

And hence 'I TAKE CHARGE!'

Signature

- Do not go forward unless you have signed your pledge.
- Signing it will crystallize your commitment.
- Read it once every morning for at least 21 days to etch it on your subconscious mind.

CHAPTER FOUR

PLUG INTO THE REAL POWER SOURCE

"'All of our behavior results from the thoughts that preceded it. So the thing to work on is not your behavior but the thing that caused your behavior, your thoughts.'
- DR. WAYNE DYER"

STANLEE'S SUPERHUMANS – THE SERIES brought to us stories of people with superhuman powers. You'll agree that across the generations we have always believed in supernormal powers.

Many people go through experiences which are beyond reason. The smallest of all for instance – thought transference. Think back to a time when you had an idea and even before you could voice it, your friend uttered it.

And you must've freaked out, "Hey, I was just about to say that. You stole my words."

The question is: Did he really?

Here's what happened. He didn't steal your words. He actually got a momentary access to your thought, that is, your mind.

Yes, in some mysterious manner, if his mind hadn't got in sync with yours, how in the world could he have uttered exactly the same words?

Stop and think.

And some of us must have experienced this phenomenon over a dozen times in our lives. Isn't that unique about our mind? Sadly, we have been brainwashed to ignore such incidents as mere coincidences. Else we are mocked at by the otherwise educated society around and we also risk our sanity in looking at life differently.

The point is: isn't that a power of mind? Maybe you've taken it for granted but isn't this how we miss the real substance of life?

As you read the two personal experiences I am about to share here, you'll begin to acknowledge the power around. I invite you to recall some of your own experiences which you might have taken for granted and buried in your memory.

Here's the first one. It's about...

...My Encounter with a Clairvoyant

In 1995, I heard about a slight, quietly-spoken woman who lived in a village by name Palavoi of Guntur district (Andhra Pradesh-India). She had made quite a name for her clairvoyance - ability to see future or past events.

She was known for her abilities to make accurate predictions. She was extremely popular for her accurate mind-reading ability and exceptional skills of peeping into someone's past, present, and future.

"She has never gone wrong," quietly whispered the local villagers on my personal enquiry about her.

All that I heard about her intensified my curiosity to see her. Finally, on a chilly winter morning of November 1995, I went along with my father to see her. Both of us had something to ask but what we got from her was way more than what we were prepared for. She exploded us instantly.

First, here's why we visited her.

My brother had been missing for over a year. There were no traces of his whereabouts and my father was curious for an optimistic revelation about his traces. As far as I am concerned, I just wanted to test the accuracy of her mind-reading ability.

The moment Amma (as she was locally popular as) saw us, she asked who Ramana was. Shockingly for us, it was my father's name. What exactness!

Even before we could absorb that, she shot one more at us, "One of your two sons is missing and his name is Raju. Am I right?" she asked. Undeniably right she was!

Wouldn't that be enough to quell our doubting minds?

We were left dumbfounded staring at each other in sheer disbelief. This was my first encounter with such power of human mind. 'Unbelievable!' was the only word I thought to myself.

She then went on to reveal a number of facts about our whole family and financial situation. They were accurate beyond a speck of doubt. It was as if she had gained access through some invisible camera into our personal lives.

She then spoke with me in private, and made some startling disclosures about my personal life which were known only to me and my friend, who was about 180 kilometers away. No chance of any prior information.

'Unbelievable!' I mumbled to myself again. I stood truly shaken to the core at how she could peep right into my past as if she had a magic telescope attached to her eyes.

She even revealed the name which was given to me at my naming ceremony. None except me and my parents would even have a chance of knowing it. My name was later changed to Ranjan Kumar. My original name was almost buried in time and forgotten in our minds. Here she was again vindicating her claim of being perfectly able to peep into our past.

We zipped our lips shut in utter disbelief.

Several days later, I went to see her again. I assumed I had been deluded somehow at our previous encounter. This time I chose to disbelieve myself. I took my friend Rama Krishna along.

Even on this occasion, she came out amazingly victorious. She seemed to have a direct pass into our minds.

After a few more interactions with her I began appreciating the hidden powers of mind. We might not aspire to develop clairvoyance as in her case but it certainly exposes the limitlessness of the powers of human mind. Agree?

Let this all sink in for a moment.

Because as you go further and further into the book you will find that you're a treasure vault of mystical powers. Once you find the key to open it, you will astonish yourself at all that you've been gifted within.

And the key is to explore your...

...Mind – The Mysterious Island

"*"And now you are and I am and we're a mystery which will never happen again."*
– E. E. Cummings"

I want you to think about the word MIND. Although hundreds of scientists have devoted lives to decode it, mind remains a mysterious island.

For every new discovery unanimously accepted in the scientific community, there are more than a dozen seeking attention.

This reminds me of one more such incident. This one introduced me to a fresh dimension as a human being. I had just returned from Hyderabad (India) after an exhausting emotional disturbance. It had almost ruptured my 'self'. I was devastated and somehow dragged my feet into my bedroom, flicked the switch of light off and dropped flat on my bed. The room was pitch-dark. It had all its doors and windows already closed. But what was to unfold in the next few seconds would transform my life forever.

To me, it was...

...My Near-Death Experience

One afternoon in February , 1997 within moments after I had closed my eyes, I felt a thousand watts electric bulb shining on my eyes. It was bright and blinding. Imagine the sun shining on your face. It was brighter than that. Even with closed eyes I felt momentarily blinded.

In addition, this was accompanied with an unbearably ear-splitting noise like that of the waves of a turbulent sea. I felt as if it was going to tear the walls of my eardrums. I did not have any feeling of existence of physical body or the surrounding at all. I lost complete sense of the world around. I felt as if I am about to split up with my physical body.

It seemed to me that I was only a moment away from departing for the unknown dimensions of the universe. But somewhere in the remotest corners of my mind, I feared my permanent departure.

On the one hand it was almost over for me and on the other hand I felt as if saying, "Hang on – I am not quite ready."

Probably I was hanging on tight to life. I felt as if my life cord was just about to be severed.

However, the little conscious 'I' that was still hanging onto the life around finally snapped. It was as if that little 'I' within was determined to come back to life.

With a sudden jolt, I snapped out of sleep. And the instant I opened my eyes I found myself back in my pitch-dark bedroom which was absolutely silent. So silent even a drop of pin would have sounded explosive. All this happened in less than a minute and life was never the same again for me.

Maybe I accidentally slipped into an unknown dimension of consciousness. And maybe I wasn't ready for it yet. But one thing was real – I woke up!

I woke to the fact that there is more to life than meets the eye. It turned into...

...My 360-hour Meditation Marathon

The experience turned out a bolt from the blue. Unknowingly I felt drawn towards silence, isolation, and meditation. As if life had just initiated a journey, I began my trip within.

I began meditating for 3 to 4 hours a day. Deep down, I knew that this wasn't something that I had picked up from outside. At the same time, I knew that some mysterious force drew me inwards.

For the first time, I woke up to life that I had ignored so far. Surprisingly, the realization dawned only once I closed my eyes to meditate.

3 to 4 hours of meditation for the next 3 months would teleport me every day to the dimensions I never knew existed. I got to experience my newer self and I turned an interesting subject for my own quest. All that I wanted to know was about me.

The journey seemed eternal as it revealed something new every next day. From unconsciously drifting in life to living consciously moment by moment, was an awakening into mindfulness.

For me it evolved into...

...My Eternal Quest for Truth

Soon I found myself reading lives of saints like Sri Ramakrishna Paramahansa, Swami Vivekananda, Sri Ramana Maharshi, Sri Sai Baba (Shirdi). I began devouring literature by Sri Aurobindo, Annie Besant, J. Krishnamurthy, Osho, Meher Baba, Paramahamsa Yogananda, etc., mining for some unknown validation for the experiences I had been through.

For the next three months, I went around searching for the explanation for what had happened with me. I scoured across books, literature, and people. They would initiate me to the different dimensions of life.

And then I came across a book which appeared as an answer to most of my questions, Living With Kundalini by Gopi Krishna. I devoured it in a day and read it again for at least 5 times.

The book became my compass and I began noticing some recognizable changes in my daily life – high self-esteem, search for meaning, deep appreciation for life, radical forgiveness, intense desire to learn, and heightened intuition. All this started shaping my new personality and changing my outlook on life.

My speed of reading doubled and level of comprehension quadrupled. Though physically I appeared frail and weak, I was brimming with energy inside.

I realized I had already set on my way to explore what India had already developed as a science, ages ago. I also learnt that such powers of mind, though extraordinary, are natural, and function under laws just as any other laws of science.

The desire to know more about the extraordinary aspects of life triggered in me the desire to go into a long spell of isolation, away from family life.

And I launched into...

...My Journey Within

In the monsoon of 1997, I left my family, hit the road, and set out for Sri Ramakrishna Math (Spiritual Organization of the Indian saint Sri Ramakrishna Paramahamsa and Swami Vivekananda) at Hyderabad.

I remember thinking: "What exactly am I headed for? And who's steering my life?"

The answers seemed to be waiting for me in time and space. I quickly realized that I was on a journey of lifetime. Once I reached the math, I met the then President Swami Sri Paramarthananda who introduced me to the Vice-President Swami Srikantananda. Intrigued by my desire to experience a monk's life, they insisted I rethink about my decision. I persisted for over two hours and persuaded them to accept my entry.

Finally, they understood my commitment towards my quest for inner life. Soon, Swami Paramarthananda arranged for a meet with Swami Ranaganathananda, the then International Vice President - Sri Ramakrishna Order.

Even as I entered into Swamiji's room, I saw him, 89 years old but sitting upright with legs resting on a chair in front, deeply engrossed in reading.

After a 5-minute conversation, he blessed me with permission to join as a bramhachari. I never thought this would be one of the most transformational times of my life. Days would start with morning prayers, meditation, and reading. Then I would rush for my additional services at the bookstall.

With thousands of books around, and a few buyers coming off and on, I had plenty of time to scan through the books. I began feasting on them binge-reading along with hours of meditation.

The experience was opening me up to a newer 'I' – the authentic self-leader within. I fell in love with the theme of self-discovery. Time spent in self-reflection prepared me for many more experiences I was yet to encounter.

With my membership in the Vivekananda Library, I started devouring books of various genres and eventually got initiated into the mind-thing through the books of Joseph Murphy, Jose Silva etc., and grew curious to explore them for a first-hand experience.

Sadly, soon I could feel the emotional pull back towards my family. With my older brother who mysteriously went missing, and my parents left with none to take care of, I felt the need to rejoin my family. Or might have been a solid excuse my mind used to convince me to retract from the monk's life.

Although I rejoined my family, my stint as a monk had already exposed me to life beyond the physical. I was convinced beyond doubt that mind is the most mysterious dimension yet to reveal its final. It became clear that it would be one of my most adventurous journeys if I could gain access to the hidden treasure.

The question I asked myself was, "Am I game for it?"

And my heart said, "YES, I am!"

Thus I began believing that the mystery of life lay in understanding the functioning of...

...Mind: Beyond Time and Space

> "*"This mind is the matrix of all matter."*
> *-Max Planck (The Father of Quantum Physics)*"

Inspired by Vivekananda, Nikola Tesla began to look at the universe as a symphony of vibrations and waves. We, in India, have had a long history of sages and saints who personally acquired and demonstrated many extraordinary powers.

It's quite obvious they left a message that human mind is the real treasure chest of all powers. From most studies later in parapsychology, we also learnt that in some unknown ways, we are connected to everything in this universe.

Put simply, our mind is a fragment of a universal mind - a pool of all minds that have ever been.

We have accepted through experience that all that exists is nothing but energy vibrating at a certain frequency. All life is energy at its core. If you hold your thumb in front of your eyes, what you see are flesh, nerves, blood, cells, protons, electrons, and finally energy. Everything can be brought down to one word – ENERGY!

Now, close your eyes for a second, and imagine yourself at a place you had visited sometime in the past or would like to visit sometime in the future. I want you to feel deeply as if you're there. Take a minute, do it and come back.

Saw it? Felt it?

Now ask yourself: How long did it take it in your mind to be at that place?

Isn't this a wonderful faculty of your mind? No kidding! You just did something which is not possible to any other species. You are unique and special, believe you me!

Now close your eyes once again, go back to a time a few years ago, and visualize something that happened with you. Recall an incident that happened to you then.

Done? How long did it take you to travel there? How did you travel time? The question is, what better time-travelling machine can we possess?

The point is, how long can we afford to ignore such unique faculties of our minds? Take a deep breath and think.

Thanks to this amazing time-travelling capacity one thing is very clear - we are not limited in our potential. You can look back at or forward to something uplifting and good at your own will.

Okay. Back to the point. You just travelled across distance and time in your mind. Didn't you? Tell me, could you have accomplished it without being connected in time and space?

To my way of thinking, everything in this universe is connected. The truth is that you don't have to believe something you already have experienced first-hand.

Point to remember: The universe is mysteriously unified and we're all connected.

Hence, even the space that you think is a vacuum is full of some substance. Let's call it thought-stuff. This thought-stuff is the most basic material that keeps all our minds connected, and helps create all that we see around and flows across distance.

More importantly, it's available everywhere at the same time. That's exactly how we are connected at an energy level.

Finally, get this - mind is beyond time and distance. It's a universal tool of power which you can use to tap and unleash...

...*Your Power to Influence*

""The true purpose of education is to make minds, not careers."*
– William Deresiewics "*

How often have you seen people who are highly qualified, well educated, yet make little influence upon the people around?

And then there are some who never went to school, had no formal education, and yet are extremely influential. They have tremendous impact on you when you talk to them, or even are close to them.

Such is their influence that they can bring massive shifts in your perceptions by their mere presence. Where does this charisma come from? How is this possible?

The simple answer is they have extreme control on their minds. They have so well tamed their mind that they seem to have command over anything that happens in their lives. The truth is that all this always comes from within because they have command on how they respond to life. Not from any external source.

FACT: It is our inner qualities of mind and character that have always given us a quantum leap in evolution. Each time a giant personality happened on this planet, life took a giant leap in its evolution.

So if you wish to influence life around, you must begin by training your mind. Your power to influence lies within when you are in sync with the universe. And you can achieve this only when you choose to employ your internal tools appropriately.

How?

The exercises in the companion copy of this book, You.2 – A Crash Course In Authentic Self leadership will help you do this.

It will also help you draw the real essence of...

...*True Education*

> *"'An educated man is not, necessarily, one who has abundance of general or specialized knowledge. An educated man is one who has so developed the faculties of his mind that he may acquire anything he wants, or its equivalent, without violating the rights of others.'*
> *– NAPOLEON HILL"*

Unfazed by his lack of formal education, Leonardo da Vinci was driven by his own code of survival and success. He went on to build an extraordinary legend and created timeless masterpieces of thoughts.

"It is only the mediocre pupil who does not surpass the master," writes Leonardo. That's how deep his commitment to learning was.

While you get to the core of real education, I have a question for you, "What is the ultimate goal of life?" Undoubtedly for me, it is to grow, expand, and become what we are built for. And this is not possible until we educate ourselves on the deeper aspects of life. Agree?

Indian yogic wisdom, long back gave us the laws of tapping the finer forces of mind. People in India have been practicing them in one form or the other from time immemorial. In fact, they are inextricably linked with their traditions and rituals.

Now here's the most important thing: Once you learn to tap them for superior purposes, you begin to grow from within instantly.

It's not what you get at the end that matters. You may get your dream job, your dream house, your dream car and even your soul mate. All this is possible. But it's who you become in the process that matters. This is what education in its true sense is.

I once heard about a magician who could make a running train disappear right in front of hundreds of people watching. When asked how he could do it he would answer, "I have full control on my mind. And since I have full control on my mind I have full control on all the minds around. They just see what I let them to see."

It might have been just a story. However, the truth is those who have better control on their minds are more influential than those who don't.

Education that draws the truth from within is everlasting and authentic. He who understands his mind gets access to his own future.

Say hello to real power!

The development of biological science has helped us speed up the growth of plants. In reality, the speed of life has increased because of the evolution of thought. What used to happen in a thousand year span became possible in a few centuries in the industrial era. We might do all of that in less than a few decades in this era.

Here's what we must remember: all evolution happens by laws. Everything that is physically manifested is based upon a medium of law. Laws are like guiding principles. What makes them universal is that they stand true for all things including you and me. Therefore, what you need to tap the power in these laws is the forward-facing...

...Efforts for Better Results

 ""*All that we are is the result of what we have thought.*"
 -The Buddha 623 B.C.E"

Indian history has hundreds of instances of yogis who could create and disintegrate things at will. Paramahansa Yogananda shared many such experiences in his 'Autobiography of a yogi'.

There was a sublime message beneath all these demonstrations. The message was to understand the underlying principle of oneness. It's a unified field of creation and we fundamentally are one with everything.

However, won't it be too shallow and highly skeptical to demand someone to prove these powers at a snap of your fingers? Allow me to ask the skeptics and the self-appointed critics a question. How many years does it take to study an engineering or a medical or a scientific course?

Has it ever revealed its final? Has it ever been understood without the ability of the person who chooses to understand it?

See the point?

Then why do we expect to understand the powers of mind so hastily – something that has never revealed its final. One need to have an open mind while seeking answers to life-changing questions. See the truth?

The quicker you do it, the sooner it turns real for you. Your sustained efforts matter more than your ability to do it. With every bit of action that you take towards personal leadership, you step closer to your higher version.

Remember how persistent you were as a child? You wouldn't stop until you got to the depth of it. You wouldn't stop until you knew it better. It's very much the same curiosity you need now to connect with your inner self.

You don't need to become a psychologist to be able to do that. It's just the way you enjoy using your mobile phones, computers and all the modern gadgets. You don't have to know everything about how they are manufactured, to be able to use them. All you need to know is how to operate them and how to have them serve your purpose.

You decide what you are going to do about it. Sit answering meaningless questions? Or start doing something valuable? Re-live your past? Or take charge and create what YOU want.

Once you decide, this book is all for you. Using the simple techniques given in the next chapter will help you gain better control on your mind.

As you reach the last part of this chapter, you'll agree that taking full responsibility to do what it takes needs you to understand...

...Whose Choice Is It?

" "The progressive development of man is vitally dependant on invention. It's ultimate purpose is the complete mastery of mind over the material world, the harnessing of the forces of nature to human needs." - Nikola Tesla 1919 "

What you are going to read next is most important. Read it, meditate on it, and understand it to digest it fully before you go further.

We have all heard life started evolving from water and in lower forms of creatures. It took billions of years for life to evolve as humans. It was a natural process until then.

Evolution up to the level of human being was a blind force moving onward. The instant life evolved into human form and since the evolution of mind began, it turned a conscious and deliberate affair.

Personal choice became foremost reason for personal leadership. As humans, we became responsible. That means we became 'response-able' - able to choose our response. This was a major shift in human evolution.

We now could take charge of our personal evolution by choosing our desired direction. Only we as humans have such powerful intelligence.

Have you ever seen an animal become a scientist? Only we, the humans, have created science. This happened because only we have this capacity to train and retrain our minds. Sadly we began identifying ourselves with our own inventions and soon we got stuck in our self-created worldly trap.

So what's the way out?

Take a close look at life and you will agree every research has its own approach. The training of human mind also has an approach which might differ from the approaches of any other physical and biological science. But should this discourage us from exploring something as worthy as our own mind? I believe no and I hope it makes sense.

You only have to operate in a different domain, and at a different level and there you are! You open the new vistas of possibilities for yourself.

With the same spirit of research that you employ in other sciences, you can realize your own nature because behind our small physical world lies an infinite dimension. You can become aware of it by becoming more aware of your own true nature. It is a level at which you are one with all at the core.

Awareness is the key!

Awareness is freedom!

So it's essential you exercise your powers of mind, explore all dimensions of your life, take charge, and steer it towards your wholesome development. Only and only then will you and your self leadership be of any use to the rest of the world.

Step up a gear! Make the best use of the companion copy 'You.2 – A Crash Course In Authentic Self Leadership' to identify ways to explore your truest potential and employ them to become and authentic self-leader.

The moment you act on your ideas, you speed up manifestation of your thoughts. You thus bridge the gap between your thoughts and your experience.

You have the most sophisticated car parked on your driveway. And you don't know how to drive it. Imagine. Does it serve any purpose? Similarly, knowledge is not power. It's only a possession like any other material object. It turns into power only when you apply it. You are powerful only when you succeed at applying it and getting the desired results. The better you become at applying it, the better are the results.

Read more in the next chapter to know more about the mindset you need to develop before you can fully take charge of your life.

If evolution until now was natural for you, it's going to be your choice hereafter. You decide what you choose. You decide what you wish to create. And you decide how you make the best use of the resources available.

Finally, if life is a magic show, remember, YOU are the magician!

So, chant ABRA-CA-DABRA and...

...Wield your magic wand!!!

Actionable Knowledge

Decide the next smallest action steps you decide to take to create a newer you:

1. _____
2. _____
3. _____

CHAPTER FIVE

◆

DISCOVER THE SEVEN-FOLD PATH TO SELF-EMPOWERMENT

""Hard is trying to rebuild yourself, piece by piece, with no instruction book, and no clue as to where all the important bits are supposed to go."
-Nick Hornby (A Long Way Down)"

LET'S GET INTO ACTION. Ready to tread the tricky territories of your inner life? Then you will certainly want to employ the following seven steps in designing your future because this is the only way you can get unlimited access to the power right at your finger tips. Ready? Here's the first one for you. You need to...

1. Set a Clear Purpose

Straight to the point - all the superheroes who you regard as authentic self-leaders were clear on their 'why'. They had a progressive life-philosophy and a clear purpose. They were committed to make meaning. They chose their belief system to materialize their purpose, and then strived to become embodiments of the beliefs.

Simon Sinek puts wonderfully in Start With Why how some of the world-class organizations stand different from the rest not because they bring out products different from others, but because they have a 'why' they stick to. The innovations they introduce therefore are the result of the belief they are committed to.

The secret is their belief of why they are into business. They work to materialize it in each product they create. Their products just reveal what they believe in.

Similarly, authentic self-leaders are unique not because what they do but because of the self-system they create for themselves. Their achievements are only byproducts of who they are within.

If vision is your destination and goal your milestone, then purpose becomes your compass and the life-philosophy your constitution.

So choose your life-philosophy and purpose before you set your goal. You will know how to do it when you get to the activity on how to set your purpose in 'You.2 – A Crash Course In Authentic Self Leadership'.

Let's get to the next on the sevenfold path...

2. Focus Only on 'What You Want'

The cold hard fact of life is that it's too short to waste on trivialities. I agree you don't always get what you desire. But does this qualify you to spend time brooding on what all did NOT go well? Think.

Karoly Takacs. If you've heard about him, you probably know that almost everybody in Hungary considers him a national hero. There is much you can gain from him. Read and re-read his story until you absorb it into the deeper layers of your subconscious mind.

In 1938, Karoly Takacs of the Hungarian Army, was the top pistol shooter in the world. He was expected to win the gold in the 1940 Olympic Games scheduled for Tokyo.

All expectations crumpled one unfortunate day just a few months before the Olympics. A hand grenade exploded in Takacs' right hand and it blew off. Takacs spent a month in the hospital depressed at both the loss of his hand and the end to his Olympic dream.

At that point most people would have called it a day. They would have probably drifted through the rest of their lives brooding on the terrible loss. But Takacs was not one to waste time on thinking about things he didn't like. Takacs did the unthinkable; he reinvented himself, dusted himself off, and chose to train himself to shoot with his left hand!

Man, that was incredible!

He put a right question to himself, 'Why not?'

Not willing to be taken apart by his rivals, he focused on what he had – incredible resilience, mental toughness and the left hand to train to shoot like a champion!

For months he did not reveal his intentions of comeback to anyone and practiced in secret. Maybe he didn't want his idea to be mocked at by others.

To everybody's shock he won at the Hungarian National Pistol Shooting Championship with his newly trained left hand.

The 1940 and 1944 Olympics were cancelled thanks to the World War II. This tested his persistence. However he wasn't one to yield. He kept training until in 1948 he qualified for the London Olympics. At the age of 38, Takacs won the Olympic gold. He thus set a new world record in pistol shooting.

What if I told you he repeated his success by winning the Gold Medal four years later again at the 1952 Olympics. He got what he wanted. You might be thinking what made it easy for him to repeat success.

Here's the trick: When you focus on 'What you want', you stick to the direction. It's as if you have your blinders on. Takacs recovered in almost less than a month. If he had wallowed in his misery, stayed a victim in the circumstances, played the martyr, and indulged in self-pity, he would have lost his mental edge – his 'eye on the ball'. And would have become history in no time.

Remember, he had all the rights to feel sorry for himself. He definitely could have exercised his right to feel pity on himself. He could have preferred to stay depressed asking himself 'Why me?'

On the opposite, he chose to focus on what he wanted from life but Not on what happened to him – a sign of an authentic self-leader.

The ultimate ingredient to enjoy success in life is to know how to focus on what you want. Next time you get bogged down by circumstances; choose to act like a winner. Take it upon yourself to think about how you chose to respond because that's the sure-fire way of getting what you want!

And this can be made easy when you begin to consciously...

3. Create Your Future Self-Image

"'If you do different, you will have different'
– DR. PHIL"

Just six months before the 2000 Olympics, American Diver Laura Wilkinson, fractured her right foot. She could not train under water as she had to wear a cast due to her fracture.

However, this didn't deter Wilkinson from preparing for the fast approaching Olympics. She chose another way of training herself.

Day in day out she spent hours visualizing each one of her dives. "I would go up to the 10-meter, stand there, and go through every dive in my head. Then when I got back it wasn't as if I had missed three months," revealed Laura Wilkinson.

She earned the first gold medal for a female platform diver since 1964.

Tell me, would she have succeeded had she not visualized her practice? I doubt.

Nothing else compares to what you're going to uncover a few seconds from now. This is one of the most wonderful discoveries we as humans have ever made - a mental ability to actualize the potential within. Go ahead and find for yourself how all that you experience is actually controlled by this invisible factor – imagination!

Now, what's the one thing you can never separate yourself from? It is your self-image. Put simply, it is what you see yourself as in your mind's eye. It's a mental image you carry of yourself in your mind.

Whether it is about losing weight, or improving your grades in class, or your doubling your performance at workplace, Dr. Phil says, "It doesn't start with diet, or exercise, or an intention to perform better. It starts with believing that you deserve what you are trying for. It all begins with adjusting your mindset."

How then do you control it?

The trick: Exactly the same way you formed your self-image initially. So how did your self-image form initially?

You formed it by:

- What you thought about yourself.
- What you accepted from others' about you and
- What you thought others thought about you.

And then the self-image you thus formed turned a magnet. It began to draw the like-minded people and circumstances to materialize your self-image. They concreted the image and this concreted image became your inner compass.

The subtle truth about self-image is that everything you think and do, builds your self-concept. You build it by constantly working on your self-image.

How then do you change it?

Here's how: Change your filter to change your future.

However hard you try to change your life, you won't be able to materialize it until you change the self-image within. It would be like changing the screen when the film has to be changed. Mind forms self-image mostly by absorbing others' thoughts. The good news is it also has the ability to create a self-image on its own. It uses one of its most powerful creative faculties to accomplish it – imagination.

And here's how you can tap its inbuilt power:

- Visualize future-backward of yourself in life.
- Imagine how you would like to see yourself in future.
- Visualize it to the minutest details including the lifestyle, relationships, fun trips, family, friends, professional, and everything that you wish to see yourself enjoying in your life and also what you would be doing to make it real.

The key is repetition. Repetition impresses the visualized self-image upon your subconscious. When the impressed image becomes part of your subconscious it develops into your new chosen filter.

That's it! And you get a new inner compass!

Anything you intend to do hereafter gets synchronized with the new image of 'self', and that's how you begin to re-create what you wish to experience.

Bear in mind that to create a better self-image you first need to build a no-barrier mindset.

And here's how you can...

4. Build a 'No-Barrier' Mindset

Stop and listen to your inner voice. Of course you've heard it is difficult to think beyond barriers especially in a world full of naysayers.

If this is what you still hear from inside, then sit back and see your barriers explode right in front of your eyes.

That's exactly what will happen when you learn how to build a 'no-barrier' mindset. Let me make it easier for you to absorb.

Being realistic seems to have been renamed as being pessimistic these days. Evidence? I will give in plenty. Look at the elevators, escalators, flyovers, flights, telephone, internet, mobile, and the technology which helps you connect with the world around in less than a second. Don't you see someone's no-barrier mindset behind their discovery?

Rare thinking people like you know that to build a 'no-barrier' mindset doesn't ask you to deny the barriers. Rather, it is helps you see the possibility beyond.

Put simply, a no-barrier mindset is all about thinking beyond the barriers.

Rajnikanth – the south Indian super star, rose himself from being a man of humble birth. He became the iconic film idol of countless people from being a bus conductor.

The question is, could he have done it without a 'no-barrier' mindset? I doubt.

The Indian elections in 2014 opened a new chapter in Indian political history. A person who started his life as a tea vendor went on to become the country's Prime Minister. Beyond any political affiliations, wouldn't you agree that it is the result of his 'no-barrier' mindset?

Sam Cawthorn, author, speaker, and philanthropist inspires people to use adversity as their springboard to scale greater heights in life.

In 2006 Sam met with a car accident, was hospitalized for over 5 months, and was told that he might never be able to walk. However, Sam chose to choose his life. He, despite having his right arm amputated and right leg disabled, chose to bounce forward.

The international motivational speaker who was conferred the 2009 Young Australian of the Year for Tasmania, says that there is immense spiritual power within an individual when faced with the choice to continue living as a victim, or to seize the opportunity of life.

You are wise enough to know that thinking 'no-barrier' is not underestimating the power of hurdles. On the opposite, it is to think about the opportunities beyond the barriers. It's a conscious choice to allow the child within to play with the thoughts of possibilities.

Have you ever observed a child closely? Let your mind shift back to a time when you were a child. Ask yourself what's unique about being a child?

Here's the answer: It knows no boundaries!

You too had a 'no-barrier' mindset as a child. That's exactly what you need to bring alive. Let the child within explore the possibilities once again before the pessimistic adult takes over and quashes them. Adopt a 'no-barrier' mindset and hit your restart button!

Okay. I know your logical brain is demanding how to do that.

Let's see how.

Negative emotions create a barrier-mindset which in turn limits the way you think about your success. On the other hand, positive emotions help you identify the barriers and root them out.

Each time you involve in a no-barrier act you feel a surge in positive emotions. You know it through experience. Each time you make a little progress, it triggers the brain activity and you get your creative juices flowing.

Isn't this what gets the best out of you?

To repeat what I mentioned earlier, doing the activities, which gives a surge in your positive emotions repeatedly, is the key. So keep doing them over and over again.

Identify activities which help you be optimistic, grateful and enthusiastic, and keep doing them repeatedly to keep yourself in the right state of mind.

The trick is to take one step at a time and...

5. Act on Your Idea Everyday

Wayne Dyer, the Internationally acclaimed speaker and writer, once told someone who asked him how often he wrote, that he doesn't retire everyday without having put at least 2000 words on paper.

Now that is what acting everyday on your idea looks like. One cannot be a champion without acting on ideas day in, day out. You must take at least the smallest step. Be it exercise, diet, writing, ideating, or anything. Each small step takes you closer to your authentic self, inch by inch, and keeps you marching ahead.

Here's how you can do it successfully in three steps:

i. **Assess the needs:**Identify the basic needs beneath your ideas. List your strengths and weaknesses. Find ways to further strengthen yourself and let your weak spots find exit from your memory.
ii. **Commit to consistency:**Most successful outcomes are results of consistent hard work than expertise. Make a written commitment to yourself to work on your goals on a regular basis. Once you impress the

commitment to your subconscious mind, you will begin to see the magic unfold.

iii. **Think possibility:**It's very natural to think of barriers. And get stuck up in the myriad of obstacles. Stop. Get committed to think about ways to think possibility. And all of this begins right at the door of your mind. What's more, it becomes easier once you begin to...

6. Devote 10% Of Your Time For Personal Re-creation

> *"'People often say motivation doesn't last. Well, neither does bathing – that's why we recommend it daily.'*
> *– ZIG ZIGLAR"*

Are you ready for this? The truth is: You cannot give away something you don't have. You only have so much energy. So, refueling your 'self' is of utmost importance if you wish to last longer in your quest of self actualization.

The reserves of energy and the 'will' you have are unlimited. But only when you recharge your batteries every now and then. You will learn more about building your 'will' in a short while in the chapter "Vasco-da-Gama Way to Success". All you need to do is take care that the channels of energy remain unclogged.

Remember, the challenges life presents to you can leave you physically, mentally and spiritually clogged. Physical Illness is the result of physical clogging. Stress is the result of psychological clogging. Loneliness and lack-mindset is the result of spiritual clogging.

Bible tells us that Jesus often took sabbaticals. Don't you think this might have been his message to the humanity? Taking time alone is to recharge your inner self. Take time to cleanse and recharge yourself at physical, mental, and spiritual levels.

Be it exercise, fun-trip, meditation, fasting, music, hobby, or anything. Just go ahead and engage actively in the soul-nourishing stuff. Each time you replenish yourself, you actually re-create yourself.

Sounds fun? Then what's stopping you? Just go for it!

And here's something that can make your journey refreshingly better. You need to...

7. Believe Before You Become

Read rags to riches stories and you'll find most of them base on the solid foundation of belief. It's your belief that gives you the power to stand by yourself. More importantly when the whole world doubts your aspirations. The lack of it is why you keep saying, "Not me, not me, not me" at every instance the opportunity knocks at your door.

Build beliefs before you act on your thoughts because what you believe is going to happen will happen. Your beliefs define the intensity of your passion and your action. Change what you believe and you will see change in what you experience.

Make a list of your general beliefs on the core areas of your life. Imagine what you must believe to make your dreams come true. Emboss them in your mind through repetition. And keep working on your dream life.

Remember, being prepared to receive what you ask for is as important as asking itself. Train your belief system to receive what you seek.

All this is essential if you wish to restart your life and all this is possible only when you develop a mindset that supports your desire.

Hold on! I can already see some questions popping up into your head. I know you are asking...

• How to develop the mindset?
• Where to draw the power from?
• What's the structure to support the process?

All this is unfolding gradually and will continue in the next few pages. You will have no choice but to succeed, believe you me!

The answer to your quest is buried somewhere in the lines of this book. It could be a one word inspiration or a line message to you. Keep scoring every inch, and bingo!

You'll have hit your restart button!

Actionable Knowledge

Decide the next smallest action steps you decide to take to create a newer you:

1. _____
2. _____
3. _____

CHAPTER SIX

❦

WAVE YOUR MAGIC WAND

> *" 'Be the master of your mind rather than mastered by your mind.'*
> *- ZEN SAYING "*

WHAT HAS KEPT US hooked for ages? It's fate. Despite the fact that we are conditioned to believe that we have little control over it, we have been obsessed to get the upper hand.

The idea of fate has intrigued thinkers and philosophers alike since time immemorial. We have always been seeking to tinker with our fate and seeking answer to the question: "What is the cause of my fate?"

Wait a sec.

Why don't we look at it in a different way?

Instead of digging for the cause, why don't we ask, "How can 'I' take charge of my fate?"

For eons, man has been making attempts to intervene with fate. The question that is pegged to our minds is – "Why me?"

How often have you asked yourself this question?

Okay. Here's what you must understand before seeking an answer - fate is a result. It's only a consequence. It's NOT a cause. It is an outcome that happens because of something, that caused it. You can change it only when you take full control of the cause. That's it.

How? Guess what? You have the resource readily available. It's your mind. You turn a magician with full control on your mind. The mind-expanding truths you will discover soon will help you see the magic. And if life is magic, it is YOU who hold the magic wand – your mind! It's your mind that holds the secrets to everything you can achieve.

So essentially you are going to learn how to...

... *Turn The Inner Projector On*

For years, I was dissatisfied with the results I was attracting. My health deteriorated while I sunk into depression and got punched out by fate. With years of reflection, I found that my mind is the projector that projects my fate which I experience as life.

Suddenly I realized that all that I was experiencing was a projection of my own mind. The moment I realized this, lo and behold, my inner lights came on.

Want to test it for yourself? Here we go...

A few quick questions:

1. How would you like to increase your personal value?
2. How would you like to make your job exciting?
3. How would you like to make your personal life fulfilling?

Point to remember: Much like a projector, your mind also has a reel of movie within. It's the movie on the reel that your mind projects on to the canvas of life. And like any other process the making of a reel needs certain components.

The vital components consist of all sensory information that we gather from our five senses – sight, hearing, taste, touch and smell.

What all we absorb through the five sense organs are only stimuli. Our brain then processes the stimuli and creates information for us to make use of. But the most significant point to remember is that for all the information it produces, mind still forms only the raw material for us to make use of.

Information is not something that you gather from outside. It's something that your brain produces after processing the stimuli that is gathered by the sense organs.

The key is to know that all information still forms only raw material for us to use. Hence, any attempt to change your fate is like attempting to alter the finished product without bringing any change in the raw material.

In a different sense it's like working on the projection on the canvas instead of working on the reel inside. If you're serious about making some lasting changes, you'll agree that any change in the finished product can be expected only when you...

...Give the Inner Designer Free Rein

"*'You have to know what sparks the light in you so that you, in your own way, can illuminate the world.'*
–OPRAH WINFREY"

Unquestionably, all self-leaders are experts at one thing - they know the logic behind creation. They are the designers of their own fate because they learn how to work on the movie within to create a desired outcome. They have clarity on the principles of creation and that's why they participate both as the creator as well as the actor. In short, they are the designers of their minds.

That's exactly what authentic self leadership is all about. One, who doesn't understand this, sits like a helpless soldier on his horse running wild. He rides at the mercy of his horse with neither a sense of direction nor a purpose.

Put simply, he is impulsive rather than responsive. He turns a mere spectator and finally ends up a 'slave of his mind'. It's high time you realized that the movie on the external canvas is a secondary creation. The primary one is the 'reel' in the projector.

The reality is that life is created twice - first in the mind, and then physically. So if you wish to see change in your fate, work on the inner movie first. Mere work on the external movie won't bring any worthwhile change because all external life is only a projection of your internal creation.

Have you experienced this – you think of bad incident that you experienced years ago, and suddenly start to feel emotions rolling in? Even as you evoke those old memories, you begin to experience the same intense emotional pressure. You begin to arouse the same feelings of anger, hatred, excitement, or sadness which you had felt long back. Only that you begin to feel them in the present as if you are going through them again now. How is this possible?

Let's see.

When you recall a bad incident from past you almost re-live the experience, and your emotional involvement deepens the experience. This is nothing but recreating the movie in your mind. This becomes your first step to the physical creation. The more you brood over them, the more you shape them up. Simple. See the truth?

This is why you hear people secretly say, "Why does this happen to me again and again?" The answer's simple, "You chose to re-live it and hence you recreated it."

No, I am not asking you to take the blame side of it and trigger guilt. Rather, I invite you to see on the positive side of it and acknowledge your contribution in co-creating the experience.

The secret to authentic self leadership is that you can design your destiny by taking full control of the reins of your horse – your mind. And the only way you can do this is when you actively engage in the process.

How? The simplest process is visualization.

You can retrain your mind to project a better life through creative visualization.

You can master it once you learn how to tap the...

...Creative Faculties of Mind

"*Imagination is the beginning of creation. You imagine what you desire, you will what you imagine and you create what you will.*'
– *GEORGE BERNARD SHAW*"

How do you invoke the creative self-system within? To repeat what I said earlier, you can harness the same power of mind which created your existing circumstances, and create a future of your own choice. I don't say you will be able to do it just like that. But I just want you to understand the principle behind creation.

The truth is that the projector has nothing to do with what reel is being run into it. The job of the projector remains only to project whatever has been run into it. That's it.

So it's the information that fills the reel which has to be changed. All that you experience through your five senses is absorbed as stimuli into your mind. What you watch on your television, listen on your music player, read in leisure, and talk with your friends is the stimuli you absorb into your mind. And it is the sensory, auditory, and visual stimuli that affect the quality of information your mind processes.

So the creation begins right when you choose the kind of stimuli that you allow into your mind.

Now let's consider watching television.

It's observed that within just 20 minutes of continuously watching television, mind becomes defenseless. Our conscious mind becomes dormant and our subconscious mind becomes a bungalow without a security officer. Everything negative we see, hear, and feel gets a direct access into our subconscious mind.

Eventually all this builds into our philosophy of life and then gradually, our reality. What you learn, listen, and allow into our mind in a passive state of mind becomes the raw material forming our subconscious mind. It also starts influencing our imagination. We begin replaying what we saw or heard in our mind. When repeated enough times it becomes the software inside, controlling the hardware – our behaviour.

"I was fascinated by a description of Niagara Falls I had perused, and pictured in my imagination a big wheel run by the Falls. I told my uncle that I would go to America and carry out this scheme. Thirty years later I saw my ideas carried out at Niagara and marveled at the unfathomable mystery of the mind", wrote Nikola Tesla in his autobiography.

Imagination is the most powerful yet most misused faculty of mind. This when blended in an appropriate proportion with our 'will' leads to what we create.

Faulty imagination complemented by our 'will' leads to life full of unfulfilled ambitions. We only chance your luck when we don't train ourselves to imagine the right things in the right manner.

Imagination when trained, intensified and made specific becomes Creative Visualization. Power of 'will' blended with trained visualization has been the secret of all accomplishments. Why don't you adopt the same secret to explore the self-leader within?

When you learn to tap the power of imagination, you take back the control of your mind. You take the reins of your life into your hands, choose what you wish to experience in future, and allow only those visuals into your imagination. See that?

This is exactly how you invoking the nature's best kept secret of creation. The more you accept this, the more fun you'll have creating a life of your choice. You will learn more on how to use this tool in 'You.2- A Crash Course In Authentic Self Leadership.

So keep on keeping on until you...

...RELEASE the Superhuman In You

You... Superhuman? Too good to be true? Let me tell you, "It's not." I hope I don't sound exaggerating when I equate man with his own creations like the Superman, the Spiderman or the Batman in terms of power. But that is real.

You don't realize it, but in the next few minutes you're going to learn how. This book is crammed full of information that will prove beyond doubt that you as a human have unparalleled power.

The supernormal powers of the characters we created enable them to perform acts which seem beyond human. We on the other hand have the unequalled ability to mold our personality, to design our future and to create our destiny.

FACT: The ability to live like a master comes from one source – mind. The power we possess can never be inferior to any of the supernormal powers of the super heroes on screen. After all, weren't all those superheroes our own figments of imagination? The powers they possess are a result of our own imagination, whereas ours is REAL!

Get the hang of it as soon as possible, and you will be able to use this resource to get empowered from within.

Hold on, I can hear you shout in your head...

...What Is Empowerment, For Goodness Sake?

> "'When the personality comes to serve the energy of your soul that is authentic empowerment.'
> -OPRAH WINFREY"

Hey! What if I told you that all creation is the result of the power of mind?

Your subconscious mind opens the door to the knowledge available and in doing so it empowers you to become the 'designer of your fate'. The quickest way to change your life is to understand that your mind is the best tool to empower yourself.

Okay. What's empowerment, by the way?

Meanings from most dictionaries say it is giving power or authority to somebody. Up until recently, I believed it to be the only meaning but soon found I was wrong. I understood it differently when I began studying people who took personal responsibility to create their own future.

What do you gather when you study the lives of leaders like Mahatma Gandhi, Nelson Mandela, or Mother Teresa alongside the lives of leaders like Hitler or Osama Bin Laden? I am sure you'll agree that they all were empowered in their minds.

Were they passionate about life?

"Of course they were!"

Then how were people in the first set different from those in the second? They were different in their purpose. It was their larger cause they directed their passion towards.

The master key lay in their PURPOSE.

Do you see how empowered these people were? They were so empowered that their thoughts and actions produced ripples across generations. They set examples either of humanity's biggest victories, or of worst nightmares. In either way, they were powerful.

Wondering where they drew their power from? Where else but from their PURPOSE? They deeply understood that we have limited time. It's again a different matter that some chose to leave this world a better place. And some left an indelible mark of evil. Those who chose to leave this world a little more beautiful felt it their personal responsibility towards humanity.

The question is: What sparked their inspiration?

The three questions that mattered for them were:

1. Who are you?
2. What do you want to do about yourself? and
3. How are you going to align your life with your purpose?

Try answering the above questions for yourself.

Mind is the most powerful tool to fulfill your purpose. So it ought to be only a tool. Undeniably it's the most freely available resource for you to add meaning to your life. You don't just live life. You make meaning and add value here.

Now that you realize that your life is beyond flesh and blood, would you be willing to invest yourself to become a self-leader? You know what I mean, don't you? Then use the natural power of your mind to serve the purpose of your life.

Well, this is empowerment!

People already have plenty of power in their wisdom to accomplish their goals. Real empowerment is letting the power out in the appropriate way.

And success comes when you...

... Let Loose the Tree within

""There are two ways to live your life. One is as though nothing is a miracle. The other is as though everything is a miracle."
-Albert Einstein "

Records of successful men of the past do us no favor except inspiring us onward. They leave us clues and bring alive the powers of mind.

Whatever Mahatma Gandhi, Mother Teresa and many others did in their lives do not help us in the least but to inspire us on. What they taught us was the power of purpose. What they left for us is the power of possibility and the power of authenticity.

Do you notice the fact that we are universal in spirit? Spirit remains the same - changeless and eternal. Your spirit is beyond time, space and law. It just is. If this is understood, everything is understood.

It has nothing to do with any religion. Neither with any spiritual philosophy nor with any organization. It's pure common sense and is purely and purely about life we all share together.

But unlike spirit, laws bind the functions of our mind. Everything we can create with the powers of mind has an underlying law.

In fact, every activity of mind is creation. It creates everything it conceives. Every thought takes shape of an image, and the image then transforms into its physical equivalent. Therefore, the foremost thing this world needs today is thought power serving the greatest cause of universal growth.

Let's go a little deeper. Mind creates through its faculties. It uses the same faculty that you employ in daydreaming known as imagination. It is the same faculty you can use to create your own 'dream life'.

When you train your imagination, you consciously visualize your outcome. Moreover, when you visualize your outcome, charged it with your emotions, you set the process of creation into motion.

All the information that your mind creates through your senses fortified by your will, energized by creative visualization, and complemented by your action turns a pattern.

This becomes our paradigm – the framework we live out.

Just incredible!

To make it simpler, paradigm is the basic design of your life which becomes the key to your behavior.

Put simply, it's a multitude of habits.

It's crucial you understand that a thought remains in its raw form until you translate it into action. Go back to nature for a moment. Every seed has a tree within. It is ACTION that brings the tree out. Similarly, you are an instrument of infinite power. It's your choice that makes you a fit instrument for constructive thinking; else the destructive thinking is readily available.

Your fate is a choice of your mind. All you need do is redesign it. The fact that you decided to read this book is enough evidence that you have identified the seed of self leadership within. Now deeply impress upon your mind that you're going to ACT on each idea you find here.

Hold it! I suggest you read the next chapter before you misjudge your personal ability to do it. You will begin to see yourself as an explorer on an adventurous odyssey. Little by little, you become free of all the inner shackles. All you need to do is sit back and open your mind. The secret is not in the words you are reading. It's buried in the insights you get while reading. Act on them right away.

Imagine living an adventurous life - creating everything you've ever desired to be, do, and have! You're going to do exactly this when you let loose the spirit of explorer within because that's who you're meant to be – an explorer!

I strongly believe we are designed to aspire for better. That's exactly what you will do when you take full control of your mind.

And that's how you take quantum leaps in your life.

Go on! Bound your boundaries!!!

Actionable Knowledge

Decide the next smallest action steps you decide to take to create a newer you:

1. _____
2. _____
3. _____

CHAPTER SEVEN

EXPLORE THE 'VASCO-DA-GAMA' WAY TO SUCCESS

"Judge not that ye be not judged"
-JESUS

ON 20 MAY 1498, a rare expedition introduced to the world one of the greatest figures in the history of exploration. It took decades of failed attempts, costing thousands of lives and dozens of ships lost in shipwrecks and attacks, to make a historic discovery. And finally one great explorer who was not willing to yield discovered the way to India – Vasco Da Gama.

It's believed that only 54 of about 170 who had left on this expedition returned. Unless someone is willing to die on his exploration, one could never leave on such a life-threatening voyage. Agree? Because it's still said to be the longest ever to this day.

You probably know that his first trip to India is considered to be a milestone in the world history. Much as I am amazed at the magnitude of this discovery, there is something else that interests me.

The question which I asked myself was, "What made him who he was?"

If you start listing the thoughts that would attack one when risking life at job, it would be endless. But what kept him driven? What kept him motivated at heart?

It was his intense desire to explore beyond judgment. At any point, he could have surrendered to the internal critic and could have convinced himself to back off. Did he do that? You have the answer. Rather he persisted until he succeeded.

The question is what made him persist. I see it this way. He persisted because he was not an explorer only by profession but was a REAL explorer at heart. He was an authentic self-leader. He wasn't doing just for a hike in his salary or the next promotion.

May be that's why it led to this historic discovery. It's not what he discovered that made him a superhero. It's his spirit within to explore - to explore the unknown!

Every moment in life we judge almost everyone and everything around. Be it in studies, at job, or with family, we tend to be judgmental every moment. The moment you realize the importance of living with a non-judgmental attitude, you see quantum change in how you experience life. That is when you begin to see life from an all-new perspective and that's how you get the 'Vasco-da-Gama way' to create your life - a life ever refreshing!

Stop being judgmental and you will take a major leap towards actualizing your potential. Your judgment of a person, self, or an incident is a mere evaluation. It's just estimation or an opinion, but when you conclude it by granting it a label, you end up judging the personality or the incident.

An African king had a close friend. He had a peculiar habit of remarking "This is good" about every incident. One day the king and his friend went hunting. The king's friend loaded a gun and handed it to the king. Unfortunately, he loaded it wrong and when the king fired it, he blew off his thumb.

"This is good!" exclaimed his friend.

The Kind was appalled. "How can you say this is good?" asked the king furiously and put his friend in jail.

About a year later when the king went hunting by himself, cannibals captured him and took him along. They were happy to have found a good meal. They tied his hands, stacked some wood, set up a stake, and bound him to it.

Just as they were about to set fire to the wood, something unexpected happened. One of them noticed that the king didn't have a thumb. Being superstitious, they never ate anyone who was less than whole. They set the king free.

Ashamed of what he had done to his friend, the king rushed to the prison to set him free.

"You were right, it was good," the king said.

The king narrated what had happened with him to his friend. About how the missing thumb saved his life. He went on to add, "I feel so sad that I locked you in jail. That was such a bad thing to do."

"No! This is good!" responded his friend delightfully.

"Oh, how could that be good my friend, I did a terrible thing to you while I owe you my life".

"It's good," repeated his friend, "because if I wasn't in jail I would have been hunting with you, and they would have killed ME."

Forming judgments is a spontaneous process. At almost every point we find ourselves making judgments. However, you're intelligent enough to know that judgment is a reaction. Not a response. It is an outcome of emotional reactivity. It's crucial you become conscious of your judgmental thinking and develop the ability to think non-judgmentally. This can happen only when you first unthink whatever you have thought so far, and rethink in a way that you engage with a new meaning that takes the context into consideration.

The real test comes during a crisis or under pressure.

As children, you must have faced the brunt of your parents' anger or frustration. Their judgmental words would've come out in the form of words like "right", "wrong", "fair", "unfair", "ignorant fool", "idiot", "should", "should not" and the likes.

Here's what happens over a period of time. The more you are exposed to such words the more you absorb them into your personality and thereby into your behaviour.

Whoa, hold your horses for a sec!

If you're asking, "How can someone criticize without using such words?" Here's your answer: Of course it's possible to criticize without humiliating or condemning but it's often hard to retreat from the process of judgment once it has begun.

To put it in Bertrand Russell's words, "I am firm. You are stubborn and he is a pig-headed fool."

It took me years to overcome the awful feelings I was stuck in due to the judgmental words harshly hurled upon me. They made me feel small as pigmy, belittled, insignificant, and worthless. I started believing I didn't deserve good things.

This had left my self-esteem badly ruptured. Any expert will agree that the effect of ruptured self esteem is sure to go deep. So before it does you need to...

...Unshackle Your Authentic Self

There is no come back to a harsh judgment. It's one of the chief reasons that distance you from your inner self because the judgmental attitude prompts you to form labels.

You start labeling yourselves by the names of your traits. You begin identifying and labeling yourselves as technocrats, intellectuals, smokers, talkative, absent-minded, ignorant, stupid, fool, and on and on.

You know what I mean, don't you?

Remember, "I drink" is not the same as "I am an alcoholic". The first one describes your actions while the second one identifies you with the activity.

NOTE: I don't endorse alcohol in any way. I don't mind as long as you don't invite me. I am done with it.

This is trivial when compared to "He is a criminal" and "He committed a crime".

The first one encourages you to think "Why isn't he in jail", whereas the second one wants you to think, "What might have happened?"

NOTE: I don't endorse crime too. However, I don't mind if you've had your shot at it, and are here to see the other side of life. You are welcome.

Similarly, if you fail to do something doesn't mean you're a failure. It just shows you need to try some other way.

NOTE: Feel free to try your luck. I have had my share of it.

Years ago, I joined a school as a teacher. I've always been a passionate teacher and kids were enthused by my style of teaching. I used to make my classes entertaining for kids with fun-and-learn method.

Once, just about twenty minutes into the class, a little boy Anil walked towards me pointing something on the board he couldn't understand. As he walked towards the board asking loudly, the principal stepped into the classroom and shouted at the top of his voice, "You idiot, you could've asked this from your own place?"

"Horrible," I said to myself. The incident rattled me to the core. Even before I could intervene, the principal had disappeared.

Moments later, I watched the after-effects of the incident on Anil's face. I picked him up and inquired and what he asked me pegged in my mind forever.

He asked, "Sir, am I really an idiot?"

See the immediate effect? It was exposed to me first hand. Judgmental words confine the whole universe to the limitations of our thinking. The reality is that our judgment can never be final because our capacity to think is flexible. Our perceptions do change and at a later point in time, we might reconsider our identification with the labels.

If you think we're hard-wired to think judgmentally, you will be excited to discover that it takes only two seconds to start thinking non-judgmentally.

Here's what you can try doing: The moment you come face to face with someone, say it aloud in your mind – I wish you well! Love is the best antidote. Try this a few times and you will see change in how you treat people.

So to grow beyond the judgmental thinking is a prerequisite to becoming empowered from within.

And here's how you can...

...Become a Self-Empowered Person

When you are self-empowered you become aware that you are a process. The key is to know that you aren't a finished product. It is to understand that labels or brands can prove detrimental to your progress because labels make you feel like products.

On the opposite, when you start seeing yourself as a process you stop being defensive. The point is you don't have a rigid structure to guard. You now are free! Not bound by defined boundaries of your traits. Imagine.

Any judgment you hold about yourself will influence your thinking. It's inevitable and it certainly reflects in what you speak, believe, and do.

This also becomes a deciding factor in how you pursue your goals because it prevents you from being authentic. It undermines your personal growth. If you're stuck in the belief that you don't deserve the best, you will never ignite your desire.

The very idea of judgment narrows the scope of the whole context of why we are as we are. This prevents us from reaching the cause. All through life we are conditioned to judge, discriminate, and brand with labels.

We start labeling the world around us in the same way it had labeled us since our childhood. We live in reaction because we tend to imitate or retaliate. The tragedy is that this continues as a never-ending cycle and the only way you can end it is by taking full responsibility of your thought process.

Everyone knows you become judgmental about yourself when you don't accept yourself unconditionally. It's the breeding zone of arrogance towards life because it doesn't allow you to accept life as a process.

Now, don't confuse accepting unconditionally with indifference. Accepting unconditionally doesn't lower your interest in self. Rather, it makes you more tolerant towards your flaws. It helps you open up more to yourself.

You can fully accept a situation or a person only when you don't resist, judge or label. Only then can you extend the same kind of understanding to everything and everyone.

It's only when you overcome your judgmental attitude that you become one of the ...

...The Catalysts of Universal Growth

All transformation we've ever seen has been because of the actions of non-judgmental self-leaders. They are true catalysts of growth. All our greatest change makers lived their lives in a very non-judgmental manner. And the easy way to create positive change is to emulate those leaders.

Let's consider one more example.

"Oh no, I'll be late to work again," How often have you screamed in fear?

How often have you tricked yourself into racing against the clock which you had intentionally set a quarter fast? You had done it to avoid any unjustifiable delays to office but your mind started believing it soon.

You get so used to it that you find it hard to remind yourself the true time. Similarly, all your judgments are contaminated by your own prejudices.

Here's the reality: the universe can neither be good nor bad. It just is. Only thoughts can be judged as one or the other. What this all means is that every judgment can weigh heavily on your perception of life.

Your judgment is nothing but a limitation - one that your mind imposes on your reality. The moment you judge, you stop being open. You stop accepting things as they are and life as it is.

The question is how you can prevent it from ruining your life. How can you totally undo the effect of judgmental attitude on your personality?

The right thing to do is raise your self-esteem. There is no other way you can do it. It helps you erase the impressions forced upon you and undo the effect of judgments from others.

So what are the easy ways to raise your self-esteem.

Let's talk about the...

...Techniques to Revive Your Self-Esteem

No surprise why Creative visualization and affirmations are the best tools to help reinvent yourself because they can easily help you revive your flagging self-esteem.

Invest 5 minutes a day visualizing how you would live your dreams if you had no limitations. Spend another 5 minutes using powerful affirmations to change your self-talk and see the magic take over!

Use your first 5 minutes of the day right after you wake up to visualize people and things you are grateful for or visualize what you wish to experience or visualize yourself doing or practicing what you wish to do.

Learn ways to train your visualization and you will have begun to see an improved life in your mind before you experience it physically.

Studies prove that there is no difference between the brain activities while you dream in sleep and while you are day-dreaming. They are the same. So your brain functions almost the same way while you are visualizing about your dreams as it docs while you arc dreaming in sleep.

You probably know how important it is for us to dream. Studies have already proved that people who are not allowed to dream during sleep can develop suicidal thoughts in just three days.

"When I'm planning on doing something challenging, I spend the time sort of visualizing what the experience will feel like...," shared Alex Honnold, the only person to have free-soloed 3000 feet high EI Capitan, with Tim Ferris on his show podcast.

Conscious visualization can help you elevate your state of mind to that of dreaming and help your brain processes your dream-life for you. The best time to do it is even before you wake up and open your eyes. Do it as the first activity of the day and see the change.

Dr. Joe Dispenza, author of You Are The Placebo: Making Your Mind Matter says that he spends about 2 hours in the morning preparing for his day, in his mind.

One more activity of your brain, which goes almost all the time unnoticed is that you are talking to yourself non-stop while you are reading this book or listening to me or doing your dishes.

That little voice going on inside your head constantly talking to you, in the scientific community, is called sub-vocalization or self-talks. Your brain in fact can speak four times faster than you can orally. This goes on the whole day and by the end of your day you have almost 50000 plus self-talk.

What the heck are you talking about? Haha.

Remember every single thought that you release leaves a chemical signature behind. It's been found that almost 80% of self-talk is negative in most cases. It's all about your limiting thoughts, and every limiting thought leaves a chemical signature in your brain.

OMG!

So the only way out is to change your self-talk. Observe what you are talking to self, identify what feelings they are leaving you with, and fill your mind with positive self-talk, consciously.

These all-powerful two techniques will not only help you feel good about yourself but also change the way you see yourself.

You might be asking, "Do we really need to feel good about ourselves." "Of Course yes!"

We do need to feel good about ourselves. At the same time, we need to stop expecting it from outside. It's disempowering to expect it from others.

So long as we accept judgments forced by somebody, we avoid taking responsibility for our own thought process. As a result, we prevent ourselves from taking charge.

Here's the bottom line: What we need is an open mind and a firm commitment to explore life without judgment. The simple way to put this into practice is to become aware of our natural tendency to judge every passing thought.

Spend at least 20 minutes every day in isolation and observe the passing thoughts without being judgmental about them. Just be. Just remain a witness. You'll be surprised how this twenty minute meditation will sharpen your observation.

WARNING: You don't need to change your thoughts. Just be available and become aware.

Awareness is the key.

Becoming aware that you are not your voice and that you are not your thought is the key. You are the one who manufactures them. You are the one who gives meaning to them. And this knowledge liberates you for the game of life.

The handy tool readily available in your hands is affirmations. Well, the problem is you might have tried a little with all positive affirmations that mostly start with the word 'I'. I am positive... I am forward thinking... I am beautiful... etc.

But if you go back to how you formed your self-concept you will discover that you formed it mostly from what you thought others thought about you were or told you about yourself. That is exactly why however hard you try to change your self-talk, it fizzles out after a while.

So in addition to your 'I am...' statements add second person and third person statements to install new beliefs about yourself. Because that is how you absorbed the thoughts about yourself in the first place.

So make some of your affirmations like I, Ranjan, am positive... You, Ranjan, are positive.. and He, Ranjan, is positive... This is what Dr. Joe Marshalla, bestselling author of Repeatlessness calls as Tri-Voice Technology.

Do you see the point now?

You can try it with meditation. Scared of the word meditation? Try sitting alone on seashore, go walking on a beach, try belly breathing, or climb up the stairs to your terrace and spend some time alone.

The motive is to be with your 'self'. It's just your ME-time. Let your thoughts run on and practice being a witness without being judgmental at all.

Initially people come back complaining that they are becoming too self-conscious. They feel tired of it – so much so that they feel like discontinuing the practice.

A word of caution: CONTINUE.

I didn't realize how valuable it was until I picked up the book, The Artist's Way: A Course in Discovering and Recovering Your Creative Self, by Julia Cameron. She advocates spending at least two hours a week in solitude. This is the most soul-nourishing activity you will ever engage in.

It deepens your ability to understand your mindset better. In other words, you become better able to engage and disengage with your thoughts consciously.

Stop pleasing others, start pleasing your soul and take time to lighten up! Because this not only makes you aware of your thoughts, but also brings your moments alive!

You will be amazed as your moments start brimming with life. For the first time you will feel alive!

Keep reading further to discover how to forge a cosmic alliance and absorb life.

It's crucial you understand this before you reap the best out of your life. And it's time you started living your dream!

Go on and say aloud, "...

Actionable Knowledge

Decide the next smallest action steps you decide to take to create a newer you:

1. _____
2. _____
3. _____

CHAPTER EIGHT

'OPEN SESAME' OF CREATION

""Knowledge comes from information- Wisdom comes from experience."
-Anonymous"

"BURY MY BODY, DO not build any monument, keep my hands outside so that the world knows the person who won the world had nothing in his hands when dying", read a forwarded message on the last three wishes of Alexander.

How true is the legend? Well, let's leave it for the historians to confirm. My point is about how you can benefit from Alexander's quest for power.

Here's how you can:

Have you noticed yet what Alexander acquired materially is immaterial in the quest of self-actualization? Because everything material can be destructed.

And you probably also know that what cannot be destructed is the learning that you gather in the process. What transforms you from within is what you become in the process. What you become sticks to your soul, and what sticks to your soul becomes your realization.

Isn't this what we are incessantly striving for?

You are intelligent enough to know that all the desire for external power merely reflects the inner need to be in control. The whole self-growth movement focuses on empowering you with the core realization that you are a being of higher order. And that you have a spiritual and mental existence beyond your physical existence.

It's extremely critical to realize that you are a spirit with mind, functioning through body. As long as you don't realize this, you will be stuck in an uninitiated belief that you are a body with some mental energy. Actually, it's the other way around. And all your attempts to realize your real 'self' are what you can call your "prayers".

What a mind-expanding thought!

Each time your prayers get answered, you get a fleeting glimpse of the connection between you and the universal energy. The continuity of results depends on the persistence of your prayers, the intensity of your desire, and the conviction of your belief.

The conviction of your belief, on the other hand, depends on the authenticity of your philosophy of life and the wisdom you gained through experience.

This follows a cyclic pattern until you internalize the fact that you are an extension of that indestructible energy, and are only vibrating at a different frequency in your body mass.

It's when you let your mind flood with this realization; you become a 'Jeevan Mukta'- a liberated soul!

It's actually fun to use the higher faculties of your mind to consciously create what you wish to experience because in doing so, you not only realize that you always had been connected with the universal energy, but also that you are the energy!

After a while it becomes more fun than need. You now begin taking delight in co- creating your life.

All you need to understand next is how you can...

...Get Plugged Into The COSMIC Hotline

"Anyone who becomes seriously involved in the pursuit of science becomes convinced that there is a spirit manifest in the laws of the universe- a spirit vastly superior to that of man."
– Albert Einstein "

'Kosmos' is a Greek word for 'order'. To get aligned with the cosmic force is to invite a life of order. It's more of an inner alignment which manifests physically as an experience.

It is freedom from dependence on external source for inner peace which takes you an inch closer to how the universe functions. Universe creates physical realities by getting thought vibrations into a certain order.

Therefore, to play your part as a co-creator, you need to play by the rules of the universe. And the primary rule is to understand that it brings order by aligning energy vibrations in a certain frequency.

In simple terms, it is to get order in your thoughts about what you intend to create. Then you turn a channel downloading the universal creative force!

If you still think that you need a car to be happy, a job to be complete, an external possession to reunite with your real self, then you are hoping to live – and aren't yet alive.

Now keep in mind I am not against the desire for material possession. Not in the least. In fact, I strongly trust that better physical comforts would equip you for larger service.

Nevertheless, if the desire arises out of a survival need, then it signifies that the connection with the universal energy has not yet been established strongly and that you're still trapped in 'existence-mindset'. You might have gathered a bunch of toys already but your mindset is still trapped in the bottom level of the Maslow's hierarchy of needs. Look within.

It doesn't mean failure. It just indicates that the wisdom gained is insufficient to become an authentic self-leader.

You live in the moment when you consciously co-create because you get into the flow. You start living for the fun of it and not for any need of survival. When you realize that you're linked to the universal energy, you fearlessly take responsibility for everything because you know within that you are only a part of the larger story.

And what's more, you also future-focus your thoughts and take responsibility for all that you'll experience in future too.

It's then that you are alive – 'Living in the Moment'!

Once you feel alive and 'in the moment', you begin to acknowledge life. Moments do not pass by without you in them. You begin to accept everything as your creation and, lo, you come face to face with the power of creation!

You start taking active role and begin to have some real fun in creation. You suddenly begin to notice the smiles around, look at the beauty of freshness in every petal, and feel complete mastery over the moment.

Therefore, what this means is that you now act from an understanding that all that has happened hitherto was also your creation. However, that it was an unconscious choice and that all that'll happen hereafter will be your conscious choice.

Think about making use of this expanded awareness.

You now don't have to wait for something outside to give you happiness. Rather you begin to emanate happiness from within. And this is exactly how you attract more joy into your life.

You now live life inside-out!

All moments and material things become your vehicle to reach your 'VISION'. Focus shifts from your need based on scarcity-mindset to prosperity based on abundance-mindset and you open up to a new realization that abundance is your true nature. There is surplus. You only need to hit your restart button and go with the flow.

And that is when you know from experience...

...Why You Are The God of NOW!

Naturally, when you start living in the moment, you are the GOD of the moment! You are 100% into whatever you do and you do this with a sense that you have the power to choose what you do..

You also know that you have the power to choose your response to the result you don't like because you start working in tandem with natural laws. Nature now becomes your partner and success is a guaranteed byproduct of this Cosmic Alliance.

Visualize a movie projector at the center of your brain and a plain canvas just behind your forehead. The moment when you feel alive, your mind begins to project the images of all the lively moments you must've experienced earlier.

Such images when projected over and over on the screen of your mind form the thought patterns and they have these images as their base. These patterns then continue to emanate thoughts of the same nature which then inspire the desired change in behaviour to physically create what initially originated in the form of thought. Thus the cycle is formed.

> ""People are always blaming circumstances for what they are. I do not believe in circumstances. The people who get on in this world are the people who get up and look for the circumstances they want, and if they cannot find them, they make them."
> -George Bernard Shaw"

As your view continues to expand, you'll find that both the brightest success and the gravest blunder start in their finest form – a thought.

Your power to choose and experience the 'moment' in the present, empowers you to choose your thought for further action. A single conscious act of decision would be enough to make master your fate! In every instant, every one of us is endowed with this power of choice and so are you!

The key is to see that 'having power' is different from 'employing it'. The moment you realize the significance of this choice, you put an end to a passive life, and launch yourself into the life of authentic self leadership!

This is when you can celebrate life, rather than hoping to live.

Now show me your confidence and continue to create a better life by learning how to...

Actionable Knowledge

Decide the next smallest action steps you decide to take to create a newer you:

1. _____
2. _____
3. _____

CHAPTER NINE

BUILD A CHINA-WALL-LIKE WILL

" "You must be willing to do the things today that others won't do in order to have the things tomorrow others won't have"
-LES BROWN"

LET'S GET REAL. SUCCESS is elusive. Look back and you will find a gaping distance between your thoughts and your action. You can also trace a gap between 'what you know' and 'what you do' with what you know.

Remember a time when you too felt the same?

Most people know that all action emerges out of one mental state – your 'willingness' to act. It's your first mental step towards materializing your idea. Your decision to act makes the fifty percent of the task done. Your willingness to take the next baby step builds the required foundation for success.

Let's face another harsh reality that success doesn't depend upon hard work. Essentially, it consists of the decision to act, a plan to stick to, and the next baby step you take towards your dream. That's it.

Do you remember the echoing words of Neil Armstrong when he put his first step on the moon – "A small step for man but a giant leap for humanity". Many believe this happened on July 20, 1969, but that's only half the story. The actual step had already been taken when it was decided to put man on moon. And the giant leap had already been taken when NASA expressed its willingness to ACT. Think.

" "Those who are inspired are willing to pay a premium or endure inconvenience, even personal suffering"

-SIMON SINEK "

In fact, the physical step was just the physical equivalent of the mental step, which combined of an all-consuming VISION and the willingness to act on it.

Take a dip into what I just said and you'll accept that each day we let thousands of such great seeds called thoughts pass by, doing nothing about them, while they wait for life to be breathed into them.

So how can you tap the energy in those seeds?

The answer is: By showing your 'willingness' to act.

Yes, it has magical power.

In fact, it impregnates the seeds of future reality with youthful life of action.

The question is: When is the right moment to decide?

Right when the seed of a vision pops into your mind.

The first few moments of the 'idea' are when you must begin to act. You express your willingness to act right when you decide to invest your time, thought, and energy into your idea.

The tragedy is most people who complain about failure are they who spend most of their time exploring reasons why they will NOT succeed. And we have been trained to call it 'being realistic'.

Know someone who does that?

Now tell yourself that success of any of your projects depend on your 'willingness to act' in the first few moments. You don't realize it yet but it's a mental habit and you can train and retrain yourselves to its mastery.

Stop and listen to your own thoughts. As long as you will keep saying, I'll wait for the right moment to act on my thoughts," you will be tricking yourself into procrastination.

The intelligent way is to act! Act Now! Because you only get one bite at the cherry in life.

The problem is when you wait for that 'flow'. As a consequence you feel stuck within. The right thing to do is to take a tiny step of action. And keep repeating it. Change often starts slowly but then accelerates quickly because when your tiny steps of actions are repeated a couple of times, they release energy and thus create the much required momentum which is powerful enough to tear open the veil around your success.

Phew! Was that too big for you to gulp?

Take a moment. Relax. Let it sink in.

But you will agree how important it is to know that your action can never be in the future because future always has its root in the present.

It's now – just this moment! Can you feel the power in your hands? Your responsibility lies in keeping your idea alive by taking baby steps and continuing until it becomes capable enough to thrive on its own. Once it gains such energy, you will have successfully aligned your idea to the universal creative force.

That's it! Rest is taken care of.

You are bound to succeed!

And at this point I know you're really looking forward to discover...

...Your D-I-A-R-E-C-T Route to Success

Your path to success begins at willingness. It's a state of mind. The question is how to develop it. The only way is to learn to 'be' before you 'do'.

'Being' has something to do with your state of mind and the key is to know that after a certain level of expertise at skill, all that matters is your 'presence'.

Your state of mind has tremendous impact on what you do because it affects your decisions. It helps you decide whether to react or respond to the external stimuli.

Have you experienced this when you are in love?

Once you fall in love, you see everything around refreshingly beautiful. As if by a magic touch, your world seems transformed. In reality, that's how you feel inside. Everything outside is a reflection of how you feel within.

One who's burning inside with passion takes every problem as an opportunity and uses it to step up the next level. On the contrary, one who is idling time in worthless complaints sees every opportunity as a barrier and thus blocks his own path to self leadership.

Now here's the reality: It's the state of mind that makes the passionate look beyond barriers and get breakthrough results! Stated differently, you probably don't have control on external factors but you can certainly invoke the desired state of mind by choice.

Isn't this exactly how most broken-hearted induce 'depression'? Isn't this how most of us have convinced ourselves to remain stuck in life by finding reasons to blame for our circumstances?

Here's the twist: In much the same way, you can strengthen your 'will' by tinkering with your mindset.

The single most important thing you will want to have is the simple framework of tools that can help you get what you want. And you get it once you grab the...

...7-Steps To A Transformational Self-System

1. D – Desire: This impulse has power unmatched by any human state of mind. Although 'impulse control' may be the last in the adolescent brain development, once tamed, this impulse can be your fuel for success.

   Just Imagine: You have been crazy about skydiving for a long time and you're all set to take a shot at it. You are falling earthward from a height of 5000 feet at dizzying speed. You can feel the chemicals in your brain kicking in and you can touch the sweat on your forehead. You have a parachute and are looking for the button that if pressed would open it. Your eyes are desperately scoping everywhere for the button and while you begin to panic you spot it. Whew!

   It is a BIG YELLOW BUTTON with words DESIRE embossed on it. Your eyes pop out as you see it. And you suddenly see the warm orange glow in the sky. You feel the desire to live a fuller life.

   How would you feel when you press it and the parachute opens? As if you just got a new lease of life, right? Wouldn't you desire to dream again? Suddenly everything seems going right, isn't it? You feel your prayers answered.

   You experience exactly the same when you tap the power of DESIRE within. And start creating what you wish to see in life. Desire is the key. It is that inner flame, which keeps you fired up to turn your dream real. Desire is your life jacket, which comes to your rescue when you are sinking deep into troubles.

   One of the greatest gifts we have is to desire to dream. Change your beliefs about desire if they are not allowing you to desire BIG. Remember, all the development you see around could not have happened without this fundamental impulse. And you certainly don't want to miss it!

   The next one is what starts crystallizing your desire. It is...

2. I – Intention: Most inventions start off with great intentions. This is a massive beginning of transformation. All until now was little vague. The

instant you INTEND to do something, you ignite the process. Thoughts begin to take form.

Intention forms the basis for the stage of planning. It brings power to your desire because it sends out a strong message to the universe that you have begun something. And you tame confusion like magic when you intend to do something.

The key is to form strong intentions before you commence your action. Turn all your wish statements into intention statements and see the magic. Take a few seconds and write all your wishes. Rewrite all of them saying, "I intend to..."

Do you feel the power in it?

Keep doing it until you turn your intentions into...

3. **A – Action:** This one step bifurcates the entire process of creation. This is the maximum distance most people travel in their journey of personal transformation. This is that mysterious juncture which most weak-minded never bound over while the authentic self-leaders push the envelope and create breakthrough results.

> *""The secret of getting ahead is getting started. The secret of getting started is breaking your complex overwhelming tasks into small manageable tasks, and then starting on the first one."*
> *MARK TWAIN"*

The good news is that you have a golden opportunity hidden within this step. The moment you begin to act on your ideas, you begin to march to a different drummer. You see life start getting clearer. The resources you need, the people who can help you, the books that can guide you and everything that can help you begin inching closer. It's as if life has turned around at a stroke.

If you are like most other people, you will still want to make your attempt fail-proof. The safe and easy way to do it is to grab the idea and act on the next possible step which will take you one step closer to your goal.

Just do it!

And keep repeating the steps. Rest assured, you will be a million miles ahead of most others who got screened out.

At this point you can stop and take a moment to celebrate. Because you just successfully made it to the top 3% of those who make this far in life.

Congratulations!

The fact that you have been with me until now is enough evidence you decided to be one of the top 3%. Further, you proved you are worth it.

Action is what separates doers from onlookers. So you now know that you are a doer. Celebrate it and take the next possible step. The question is how you can ensure success of the process.

Here's how you do it: Ask yourself these 5 questions:

1. Why do I want to do it? (Ask 7 times)
2. What's the result I want to see?
3. What's the next possible thing I can do?
4. Am I willing to do what it takes?
5. Am I willing to enjoy the process?

Now that you've answered the questions above, how do you ensure success? Read on...

4. R – Repeat: This is not going to be anything new for you because it's something we all do once we get habituated of thinking in a certain way. We keep thinking in the same way and keep repeating the patterns. And that's perhaps why we are called as creatures of habit.

What's silly is expecting different results while doing things in the same way. You can't be procrastinating things like earlier and expect different results.

Now that you have committed to act on your ideas, you've already taken a major leap. Adopt new principles, accept new values, install new thought patterns, build new habits, and adopt a new lifestyle. Repeat them until they become your second nature. That's it.

The key is to harness the power of frequency.

What you do every day is more important than what you do occasionally. Doing something repeatedly has unimaginable power.

Repetition is the key. It builds momentum.

This is one of the most important components that manufacture success. Let's look at next magic key...

5. E – Expectation: Put your palm on your heart and tell me...

Do you want to be successful? Yes?

If yes...

Do you expect to be successful?

You got it right.

Do you expect to be successful?

'Expecting' to be successful is the most important for success. You begin to act upon your dreams only when you expect yourself to succeed. You are doubly motivated only when you expect to succeed.

On the contrary, you don't act upon your goals when you don't expect to succeed. So, begin to expect success because when you do it you begin preparing for it. It's a powerful motivator only when you use it to your advantage.

Most people don't expect good because they unconditionally accept the realities given to them. If you keenly observe the people around, you will find most of them accept the circumstances they are in. They yield to the problems life has thrown at them and lazily accept the limitations.

To shift gears you must change your expectation of future. Things change only when you expect them to change. That's how powerful 'expectation' is in the process of personal transformation.

So if you feel the desire to change your future, hit your restart button, and affirm aloud to yourself, "I expect something good to happen to me today."

Repeat it every day until it sinks into your subconscious mind and let it become natural to your mind. It's only then you begin to see change in your life.

Stick to the process because it's highly important you realize the importance of...

6. C – Committing to the Process: Ask any champion and here's what they'll name as the prime factor in their success - commitment.

Yes, commitment has the power to unlock the doors to your dream life. I know what you're thinking – "Don't people already know about it?"

"Of course, they do!"

"Then what stops them from being committed to their dreams?"

"Are you ready for this?"

"They just don't have compelling reasons."

All those who succeed in creating a life of their desire have compelling reasons which get them committed to the process. You need a compelling reason to wake up an hour earlier. You need a compelling reason to work an extra hour. You need a compelling reason to reject the naysayers and you need a compelling reason to think out of the box. Especially when everybody around you thinks, you must be out of your mind. Makes sense?

So how do you get committed? Here's how... First, decide what you love to do. Second, Begin working on yourself. Finally, what you need to grease the wheels is...

7. T – Trust: Develop trust in possibilities. Trust that your dream is possible to achieve. Trust in your ability to make it possible.

Drift back to the time when you were a kid. You had infinite trust on everyone and everything around.

You trusted this world is abundant and that you can get everything you desired. You trusted that trying to reach for things you want is exciting. What happened to you later as you grew up was not the effect of the circumstances you experienced but the way you were taught to interpret them. You saw people around responding to situations and picked up the ways to interpret situations. All this happened so fast you never realized it became your mindset.

Most of it was inspired from what 'others' felt was right, and gradually they began to impress their opinions upon you. You, like a piece of sponge turned a victim of 'learned helplessness phenomenon'.

Think back to the time when you were a toddler and rising back after falling down was natural to you. How else did you learn to take your first steps? Don't you feel you could have used the same built-in mechanism to rise in your personal and professional lives?

I can feel your pain and anger because I felt the same when I reflected how long I waited to awaken the self-leader within.

And once I found my way, I had to get aligned to the universal laws. Curious what they are? And how can they help you? Ready to dive in? Here we go...

3 Steps to Strengthen Your Will

1. BECOME DISCIPLINED

Discipline. How does this word sound to you? I'm sure it's the most negatively perceived word. To most people it sounds like regimentation.

On the opposite, it's different with the authentic self-leaders. Read their biographies and you'll discover that discipline tops the list of their priorities. It's the same with almost all.

To them discipline is focus of will, energy, and time. To them it's concentration of all that they have on what they want. If there is one thing you can learn from them, it is this: discipline is to focus on only things of crucial importance.

To be disciplined is to live with self control so that you don't fall prey to easy choices. Because that's the only way how you can resist temptations in all its alluring forms.

Nothing more and nothing less. The next is to...

2. LEARN HOW TO FAIL FORWARD

There has been a lot of hype for smart work. We almost have begun to take it far too simplistically. Carol Dweck in her extensive research on the type of mindset required to succeed in life concluded that there are two kinds of mindsets - fixed and growth.

The way I understood it is that people who do not change and adapt are those with the fixed mindset. They are obsessed with success but are not willing to change according to the need. They are only concerned about the result and not the process. They want miracles but don't intend to change.

On the other hand, people with a growth mindset are those who are inclined to learning from the process than the achievement. Success for them is a byproduct.

To develop a growth mindset you must be willing to fail forward. Failing forward is to realize that you learn something new irrespective of success or failure.

You must be willing to focus your mind on learning than achievement. And that's how you'll wake up to the fact that you learn even from your failures.

That's how you fail smart and yet maximize on all incidents in life. That's how you put your life on the fast track route to success because that's how the self-leaders do it.

So get this – failure is the mother of success!

Learn to embrace your failures and...

""You don't have to be great to get started but you have to get started to be great"
– Les Brown"

Lorose

3. SACRIFICE PETTY GOALS FOR THE WORTHY ONES

Hey! I know what you are thinking. "Sacrifice?" "What do I have to sacrifice?" "Only the worthless distractions that have kept you long from succeeding all these days."

Let me explain. Sacrificing things to focus on your dream is NOT to renounce all good things. You only need to sacrifice your worthless goals eating away at your focus.

If you go back to the 6th step to hit your restart button in chapter 4, you'll understand what I just said. The reserves of the 'will' you have will prove productive only when you devote them to your BIG and worthy goals. Sacrificing your unworthy goals for the worthy ones is the real sacrifice. It's a small sacrifice you do to get the BIG results you desire.

Ever wondered how you can do this?

Here's the trick: Start installing the belief that you deserve a better life. Your self-esteem is directly proportionate to the size and quality of goals you pursue. Boost your self-esteem. Use positive self-talk. Autosuggest your mind and intensify your desire to live life king size. That's exactly how you escape the pull of shallow goals.

And here's how you can stick to your endeavor: Ask yourself every night: "How willing am I to give what it takes, to make a big positive difference about myself?"

A word of caution: It's not going to be a one-shot affair. You need to answer the question every night. And what's more, you need to rate your response on a scale of 1 to 10 as Marshall Goldsmith suggests to develop accountability.

Keep doing it consistently and keep observing the response. This helps you make your 'will' seem measurable and something that seems measurable becomes achievable. And something that becomes achievable doubles the probability of success.

Remember it's all about increasing your probabilities of success because it's a probability game.

So finally, it is not the technique, which matters. What matters is: "Are you willing to act on it?"

Success lies in your willingness to act. Take the next possible step. Keep on keeping on.

And there you are – MISSION ACCOMPLISHED!

Still need proof?

Turn the page and keep going!

Actionable Knowledge

Decide the next smallest action steps you decide to take to create a newer you:

1. _____
2. _____
3. _____

CHAPTER TEN

✦

TAME CONFUSION LIKE MAGIC

"Inaction breeds doubt and fear. Action breeds confidence and courage. If you want to conquer fear, do not sit home and think about it. Go out and get busy."
-DALE CARNEGIE

EVERY DAY I WAKE up to a battlefield of two conflicting wolves. I am talking about my half-and-half self. One is my CRITIC SELF, who to me is a jumping bean because it has a bug inside - criticism. It wants to find fault with every passing idea. The other is my COMPANIION SELF, who like a buddy says, "Hey! Why don't you just believe in yourself, step forward and act on it, bro!"

You probably know what happens when you begin to act on your goals. Even before you take your first step forward, you find yourself confused. You see a terrible fight between these two wolves. The truth is that the same fight is going on inside everyone you see around. Need proof?

Here's plenty for you: Each time you begin to write a book you find yourselves confused where to begin. You decide to be fitter and begin to exercise, and suddenly you are confused what exercises to start with. You want to do some social service and are confused where to start. You want to inculcate a habit of reading and you find yourselves confused over which book to read first.

The question is: What causes this?

Let's explore in depth.

Each wolf represents a set of traits. One represents fear, guilt, inferiority, and the traits that hold you back. The other represents hope, confidence, humility, courage, and the traits that help you focus on growth.

Do you want to know how most people react to it? They do nothing. Just nothing. I too have been through such phases countless times. Most people do it. They live as if they're sitting in a cab idling at the roadside.

How do you feel sitting in a cab, the engine ticking over? You somehow get a feel that you are going somewhere. And you know the reality that you aren't.

Remember the first time you drove a vehicle? You had just too many things dying for your attention. You had the steering wheel in your palms and a hundred other details seeking your focus.

Put simply, you were confused.

Well, who would want to be in such a state of mind intentionally?

If you too dislike this ugly phase of life, then ask...

...What is Confusion?

Ready for this? It's a sign you are out of your comfort zone. A lot of people feel it's something which stops you from what you can do. But most of the times, it signals you that you have just begun to do something! See the positive side?

Confusion is good. It scares the hell out of you and tests your persistence. Yet it's good! Sounds hard?

Keep reading and you'll prove it to yourself.

Tell me: how did you feel when you stepped for the first time into your school as a kid? How did you feel when you thought of asking your boyfriend or girlfriend on a date for the first time? Confused? If you're like most people, you'll agree you were.

Well, most of us are.

Confusion precedes clarity. It's a sign of growth and movement. In fact, the absence of confusion exists only in the state of complete inaction or action. Hence if you are not in action, and yet not confused, believe me you are doing nothing.

Stop and think.

There is nothing like a neutral state. We either evolve or stagnate. But we are never the same because there is nothing like a neutral state in life when everything around us is evolving. Hence we are dying out while we aren't evolving.

The mind-bending reality is that everything that is growing is continuously creating and re-creating itself.

So fundamentally, everything is changing.

Look at the trees around...look at the people around...slow down your car and look at the shops around... Are they the same? You probably got the answer.

All creation is in a state of flow. It's growing from within. Creativity is a state, which is in harmony with evolution. Inaction is not neutral. It is not a state where everything stands still. In fact, it is dying out.

Though you might find it difficult to acknowledge, inaction is letting the whole world pass by you.

Finally, take it from me - universe has a habit of discarding anything that is not growing because inaction is death.

To make the most of your life, upshift yourself from...

...Inaction to Action

> "*I don't sing because I am happy. I am happy because I sing.*"
> *-William James*

Get real. Absence of confusion indicates you either are in the state of flow, or are in the state of inaction. Confusion is a state between decision and flow. It indicates you just lurched out of your comfort zone.

It's an impressive indicator that you are in action. You just have to keep going to gain enough momentum. Once you gain enough momentum, you get into the state of flow. And this 'flow' is a state of creativity.

Keep in mind, confusion is a hundred steps closer to creativity than inaction. It just demands your decision to act, and then to ACT. The reality is when you are confused, you either are afraid to decide, or choose to remain passive.

Now that you have seen the positive side of confusion, let's go a little deeper and study its cause.

What causes confusion?

Be true to yourself and answer, "Where has your confusion originated from? From the action you have just taken or out of your choice to remain inactive?" Time to face the truth.

Let me make it simpler for you: If you have a dream and yet choose to remain inactive, you are inviting confusion. But if you are confused because you just took your initial actions towards your purpose- Congratulations! You are on your way to success. You just stepped out of your comfort zone and such confusion is a million times desirable that the one which comes from inaction.

Confusion, as a state, has a positive and a negative side. The negative side of staying too long in this state is that it builds up its negative volatile energy. It shapes itself into a dangerous quagmire and forms a inescapable loop which pulls you inside till you yield to death i.e., inaction.

So roll up your sleeves and...

...Beat Procrastination

Here's the enemy we are yet to tackle. Do you now see that the more time you stay confused, you deliberately choose to delay your decision?

This is a period of terrible indecision. Believe me, the indecisive state of mind is the breeding zone for the habit of procrastination. What's the simple and core personal growth lesson here? The more you allow your mind to remain in such a state, the more you get entangled in the habit of procrastination.

That's exactly when you start hearing yourselves saying, "I am confused. I had better put it off for later."

Such long spells of confusion, when deliberately allowed to repeat again and again develop into personal traits of procrastination and guilt.

Guilt would develop for every action not taken because you will at some point say, "I should have done this, then." But you also know deep down that 'then' never comes back. Time never repeats itself because life is in the NOW. Yes, 'now' is the only moment you can live in. You can neither live in the past nor future. And the present is always beset with confusion.

So what can be done?

Bring certainty to your plans. Yes, future is never certain but human mind craves for certainty to take steps forward because certainty is the primary human need which influences our actions. Uncertainty leads to procrastination. Certainty gives you the ACTION CONFIDENCE.

The moment you declare to yourself with absolute certainty that, "I am going to do this!" And then start taking action as part of plan – something magical happens. Planning creates patterns. And once you stick to them, you create certainty that your mind needs to make progress. This is exactly how you begin to develop the certainty you need to live your dream.

That's the whole secret: Life always happens in the 'now', that is, this moment, this moment and just... this moment.

So to relish it fully it's not enough just to know what you want to do, but also to...

...Know What You Don't Want to Do

> ""Knowing what you don't want to do is the best possible place to be if you don't know what to do, because knowing what you don't want to do leads you to figure out what is it that you really want to do."
> – OPHRA WINFREY"

Ignorance can't be an excuse. Let's talk about why "what you DON'T know" is so crucial to your self-growth plan, and how you can start making it work for you. How does "what you don't know" affect you?

Let me share with you something hard-hitting based on my experiences.

Over 15 years ago, I went through a phase of life when I spent years in limbo. This was the time when I wasn't sure what to do. Uninterested and unmotivated I turned an aimless wanderer. Since I wasn't sure of what I must do, I turned an easy prey to people who too were aimless. The more I roamed with them, the more I picked up their ways of thinking, or not thinking. Soon their lack of ambition rubbed off on me.

I began taking life for granted, and continued to do so until life jolted me out of my deep slumber. It was painful because it came with the right dosage of damage - both in my personal and professional lives.

I woke up to one more reality of life. I realized that it is not enough just to know what you want to do in life, but it is highly essential you identify what you don't want to do.

Unless you know this by experience, you are probably shocked. At the same time, you feel incredibly empowered because once you know what you don't want to do; you easily carve a brighter future for yourself.

How often have you found yourself unconsciously doing things you never were interested in? You found yourself there just because you didn't have anything better to do. You found yourself with a group of people just because you didn't have better options.

Remember, it's a very dangerous phase of life and what you see is just the tip of the iceberg. You could end up a lost soul not knowing what your purpose is.

To reinforce further, 'regret' is the only feeling you'll be left with at the end of this phase. Guilt is the natural outcome of killing time in things good-for-nothing which steal away the opportunities of increasing your inner value.

Millions of teens could have steered their lives towards something worthy had they been trained to take charge. Imagine. If you are like me, you are wondering how we can expect something worthy from the next generations while we don't bother about helping them find meaning now.

Want to do something real to help people around?

Want to help them unshackle themselves from this trap?

Then first help them get released from...

...The Bermuda Triangle of Life

Now that you are going ahead, come hell or high water, you need to be on the lookout for the 'Bermuda Triangle' of life because even the strongest have disappeared into them and got lost to the world.

But don't forget to take stock of all the impending risks before you step out into the unknown. As noted earlier, self-leaders know deep down that there are going to be risks on their way to success. And that is why you become a hero when you get what you want from life. But they also promise themselves that they aren't going to be blindfolded to the risks. Rather, they educate themselves about them and work to minimize the risk factor. That is why we are superior to all species, after all.

Here are the three sides to the Bermuda triangle of life: Fear, Inaction and Confusion.

You probably have seen them at close range. It's crucial you protect yourself from getting trapped in. Wait a sec. If you're like most people, you hate taking risks.

Straight to the way out: Become aware of their positive aspects.

In fact be ready to flip the triangle over.

The single most powerful way to turn the three negative forces into positive is to become aware of your resourcefulness. Yes, take a U-turn and direct your full attention to the powers within. That's the only way you can get past the devil's triangle. Here's how...

The key is awareness.

The technique is attention.

Here's how you can tap the power of awareness. You can begin by visualizing the positive outcomes every time you undergo these negative feelings. Remember you cannot get new results by playing the same movie again and again. You need to create and strengthen new neural pathways in your brain. That's the only way you can create a new future.

Reframe the ending and repeat it in your mind until you see it in real. Simple but profound!

Let's get deeper to the trio:

1. Fear: An Indian story goes that there was a mouse which was always afraid of a cat. How unnatural! It sought help from a magician and pleaded him to turn it into a dog. But later it grew fear for attack from a panther and requested the magician to turn it into a panther. A few days later, it found itself gripped in the fear of an attack from a hunter.

At that point the magician realized what had been missing. He said to the mouse, "Nothing I do would do you any help because you still carry the heart of a mouse."

Quick Recap:

Do you remember this from 'Shoot The Seven-Headed Monster - Fear of failure is the biggest of all the psychological barriers?

The key is to understand that it's a learned fear which in most cases we picked up from our surroundings.

So what is it that you are afraid of?

List your fears. Public speaking? Writing? Expressing your needs? Asserting your stand? And what else?

Now's the best time to become aware that fear is only a signal from inside that you are not ready yet. It's natural because we have a system within that warns us when we are not prepared for something.

Tell yourself, it is OK not to be perfect. It is OK to be a learner, and then stretch your comfort zone and go and do what you intend to do.

The trick is to use your fear positively and to intensify your preparation towards reaching your goals. This is probably the easiest way you can get back to basics and tame your fear.

What this all means is simple: You have the choice to knock your fear flat before launching your winning blow.

But also remember it's dangerous to ignore your fear. The truth is you must acknowledge your fears. And once you acknowledge your fears you just go doing what your heart asks you to do.

2. Inaction: Imagine using your car for over six months at full stretch without taking it in for a service. How would you enjoy your ride in it?

You probably have the answer. Similar is the case with your body. Your body is a complex system which needs timely rejuvenation. When you don't allow it to replenish its reserves of energy, it might just give way. It is then that inaction sets in. You feel stuck in limbo. That is when you hear your mind asking for a recharge.

Use the time when 'inaction' sets in to work on rejuvenating yourself physically, mentally, and spiritually. Take advantage of this barrier. Spend an additional half-hour at your gym, stretch your walk schedule by another half-hour, find a different way to spend time in solitude, and try simple breathe-watching as meditation. Do something to push your limits. You're smart enough to find ways to make best use of inaction because that's the best way to bounce forward.

So stop kicking your heels and gear up to give life a surprise!

3. Confusion: Progress is always 'messy'. Confusion is an expression of your inner need to get in synch with your purpose and resourcefulness. Each time you sway from your 'major purpose' confusion sets in.

After all, how do you think your mind must let you know that you are off course? There has to be something which warns us when you go off the track. And life knows better. It is nature's perfect cybernetic substitute in your mind. This is how it lets you know that you need to get in sync.

In fact, it is a way your soul expresses its need to get nourished. And the best way you can nourish it is to align your actions with your purpose. That's it!

So, how do you align you actions with your purpose? First, it's time you understood...

... What Stops You From Action?

UNCERTAINTY. It's hidden deep in your mind. Studies prove that our mind craves for certainty. You choose to act only when you are certain. Most people act on impulses because they get to experience instant outcomes. They are certain about immediate results. However, they find it difficult to act on ideas that will get them better results in future. The reason? Future is invisible. It's somewhere far from your eyes and the result is always uncertain.

If one reason is that future is invisible, the other reason is that to create a desired result, you must work – work your ass off. NO EXCUSES. And you need to take full responsibility for all that you're going to create. No matter who you are, you get the desired results only when you take responsibility for the consequences. But this is not normal hard work because you now are inspired to act towards your purpose. So this turns fun and creativity.

The question is how you can bring certainty into your process? Simple: Planning. Yes. Planning the details of how you are going to achieve your goals can give your mind the impression of certainty. Planning is priming your mind for the future. The more you get detailed in planning your journey, the more it looks real and believable and that which is believable is achievable.

While it is not necessary that the universe respond to your plan the way you want it to, you certainly can trick your mind into making progress.

Most of all, you can beat your super psychological barrier – PROCRASTINATION. An easy way to get breakthrough results – consistently.

The key is planning.

It might not help you build a quantum-leap mindset but it can help you build momentum. As a consequence it can help you overcome the negative effect of confusion.

Further, to get to the other side of inaction, you also need to have a glance on...

... The Positive Side of Confusion

""All great changes are preceded by chaos"*
-Deepak Chopra"

Everything in life has a positive side. The positive side of confusion is that you cannot skip this state at all. All through your life. Why?

Take a close look. Life is a series of incidents and actions. For every new action you consciously take, you stretch your comfort zone by an inch. And each time you act towards your purpose, you step out of your comfort zone. You stretch it to its new limits. And that's how you create the new unstable state of mind – confusion.

The reality is, this unstable state of mind is nothing but the time your mind buys to get familiar to the new 'change'. It is during this time that it forms new neural pathways to adapt to the new circumstances. And that's how you gain mastery at the new tasks. This is a phase you must expect before you succeed.

Look back into your life and you'll find a million of such phases you must have already sailed successfully. You must have encountered them before you took your first footstep while learning to walk. And even before taking your first ride on your bike.

Do you know the reason you succeeded?

It's your conviction that you're going to succeed no matter what. It's your trust in the unknown. You might have not known 'when' and 'how'. Nevertheless, you certainly knew you are going to succeed at some unexpected moment. Or probably you weren't even bothered about success. You just wanted something and went for it.

Once you expect such periods of confusion, you also subconsciously command your mind to foresee it. And that's probably how your mind explores ways to overcome it.

The good news is that you have two wonderful faculties of mind built-in to help you speed up the process – will and imagination. You can speed up the process by strengthening your 'will' and refining your 'imagination'.

And then you begin to have childlike delight going through such phases of instability leading to a decisive action. In fact, self leaders acknowledge the fact that they will have to attract more of such states of discomfort. They find it necessary to repeatedly stretch the limits of their mind and challenge their safety net.

That's exactly how we can get ready to command our minds.

I would like to take a step forward and say, "You had better be confused than inactive."

I appreciate you for the courage you've displayed all along the way. As you stay focused you'll be amazed at the simple ways you can create a newer you.

Stay tuned for more.

Ready to roll up your sleeves?

Let's roll...

Actionable Knowledge

Decide the next smallest action steps you decide to take to create a newer you:

1. _____

2. _____

3. _____

CHAPTER ELEVEN

I DON'T KNOW - THAT'S EXACTLY WHY I KNOW

" "The greatest enemy of knowledge is not ignorance; it is the illusion of knowledge"
-Daniel J.Boorstin "

"WHO WAS THE FIRST SCIENTIST?" a child once asked Dr A.P.J. Abdul Kalam (Former President of India). After thinking for a while he answered, "It must have been a child."

In saying that, Dr Abdul Kalam was referring to the authentic inquisitive nature of a child. Do you remember how curious we were as kids? We, as if embodied the Zen principle, emptied our heads before seeking new learning.

This reminds me of the old Indian story.

There lived a king called Janaka. He was a ruler with a bent for spirituality. Once, even as he was reclining on his flowery and fragrant bed he slipped into a nap. He soon drifted into a dream in which he was defeated by another king and was taken prisoner by the enemy soldiers. He was then being tortured into giving them the royal secrets. This jolted him out of his sleep only to find himself back in his luxurious and fully guarded bedroom.

The king once again dozed off into a tortured sleep and experienced the same dream. Again he woke up only to find himself in very safe and peaceful surroundings. The experience sort of disturbed his inner peace. The dream was so real that he could even feel the sweat on his forehead once he woke up.

How could a dream be so real?

What bothered king's mind was the question, "Which is real – dream or life?"

He summoned all the elite and learned pundits of his empire. But no one could satisfy his quest. The word of king's dilemma spread like fire. One fine day, a man called Ashtavakra (deformed or crooked), knocked at his door claiming to have an answer. He claimed that he was a misfit to many domains because of his physical deformity. And so he chose the domain of wisdom which has nothing to do with his physical deformity. That is why he said he had enough wisdom to clear such doubts.

King shot his question at Ashtavakra. And he answered, "Neither of them is true". Shocked at his answer the king hurried to ask, "How could both be untrue?" And Ashtavakra goes, "When you are in the dream state, the waking state does not exist. And when you are awake the dream state does not exist. Hence none of the two is real."

King went on to ask, "Then what is real?"

Ashtavakra shot back, "There is something beyond the two. It is for you to discover. That is real."

In brief, all the knowledge in this world awaits you to discover it. You need to have a right state of mind to successfully explore the unknown. With this in mind, it's crucial you understand that knowledge exists in two domains. You discover it fast when you are aware of the domains.

So to do it successfully you also must know how to work with...

...The Knowledge in Two Domains

"*"Without continual growth and progress, such words as improvement, achievement, and success have no meaning."*
-Benjamin Franklin"

Interestingly, existence of all knowledge can be divided into two domains. One: It is knowledge that we already have acquired. And second: It is knowledge we are yet to acquire.

The question is why most people fail. Think. The single most important reason is they don't know that they don't know. And the tragedy is they think that they do.

Think about this and you will agree that all fresh discoveries are born in the 'I-DON'T-KNOW' domain. And then they begin to root as 'I KNOW'.

The fact is, nothing is ever completely discovered. This universe is always in the process of discovery. The instant something is discovered; it is on its way to decay.

In fact, all aspects of life can be classified into these two domains 'I Don't Know' and 'I Know'.

Problem arises when we are stuck for a long time in the 'I Know' domain. The 'I Know' domain is like a rock. If you get stuck in this dimension, you wouldn't want to change until nature forces you to.

Beware! When you say that you know a certain way of doing something and believe it to be the only way available, it remains the only way even if you are headed towards failure.

Want to know why?

Because you have formed and fixed the belief that this idea is the truth. The reality is that 'truth' is only a perception that continuously shapes and reshapes itself. We call it 'change'. See the point?

The fact is all change shows up from the 'I-Don't-Know' domain? In fact, you don't discover 'change'; it reveals itself. It reveals itself to one who makes himself available to the 'I Don't Know' domain.

The question is how you can access this domain.

How do you get access to this all-creative domain?

Well, here's...

...The Secret Vault of Life

" *"It's what you learn after you know it all that counts."*
-*John Wooden* "

First things first, you need to acknowledge that the domain of 'I-Don't-Know' is limitless. It's vast enough to contain in itself all the uncovered knowledge and all the probable possibilities.

For every mustard seed size of discovery made, there is an Everest size of discovery to be unearthed.

What's more, the 'I-Don't-Know' domain holds the secrets to all new discoveries. Because to operate from this domain is to move into the space of unknown.

This is exactly where you get access to the secrets of life and also to the potential to re-script your story. And this is also where you step into your 'higher self'.

Say hello to the stranger in you!

Go a step ahead and you will find that your 'higher self' and everybody's 'higher self' are unified in this dimension. Call it 'akash' or 'the ether' or 'unified field', the fact is there is some dimension all of us have equal access to and hence are unified in that domain.

Relax! Actually, these are fundamentals.

These are what we are made of. These are simple yet powerful truths you deserve to know. And that is why I feel it is your right to uncover these truths.

Don't you think you deserve to know everything that makes your life? Don't you think you'll be better able to design your life, once you get to the roots of the universal laws? You don't have to believe me, believe yourself!

Now get this - your desire to get access to this wealth of information itself is the key.

The more intense it is, the quicker you get access. So get ignited from within to become a perfect channel.

How? Simple. By acknowledging the fact that everything you wish to create already exists.

What a shift in perception!

Here's where quantum leap begins.

You just need to get in tune. Intensifying your desire to unlock the universal secrets is allowing yourself to be a channel. It has the potential to open the doors to your higher self.

It's as if you have become part of a rare group who get to see a totally different view of this world!

> *"Being ignorant is not so much a shame as being unwilling to learn"*
> *-Benjamin Franklin*

Once the thirst in you is aroused, you start finding new ways to address the same old problems. I want you to know one more thing: This 'I-Don't-Know' approach doesn't originate from arrogance or ignorance. You don't say, "I-Don't-Wish-To-Know" or "I-Can't-Know". You say 'I-Don't-Know' because you trust that the universe is always in harmony with your creativity because you trust you can expand your awareness.

And that's when you begin to...

... Think Out of the Box

The phrase seems to be giving a buzz to the youth today – out of the box thinking! Everybody knows, any new discovery is a byproduct of a certain way of thinking. And it can be best called as 'out of the box' thinking.

How often have you had a new idea only to hear your inner voice putting it down by, "Who do you think you are?", "It's absurd"...

To think out of the box is to say NO to boundaries. To think out of the box is to push the limits. To think out of the box is to stretch your comfort zone.

If you're wondering who created it in the first place, here's the answer: YOU.

Yes, you unconsciously created it from all that you absorbed from your school and family.

What then is thinking out of the box?

It is to willfully say yes to momentary confusion. It is 'willingness' to fail and yet try again. That is probably why the knowledge we gain through such attempts are called DISCOVERIES.

Cast you mind back to your life at school where most of what you learnt was how others perceived life as. Most of it was about what the world thought it to be right. That's exactly when you built your 'box' in the first place.

Being in the box is mere survival by default. It is easy. It is safe. And it is this comfort of the safety that doesn't allow us to cross the boundaries.

Do you remember the dreams you had during your childhood? You were free to imagine. You had the courage to look beyond boundaries.

Now let's come back to reality. To be anything different you must first peep out of the box. To be out of the box is to go into unsafe territory. It is to be willing to be vulnerable and absurd. You must be willing to be confused. You must go crazy about creating a new boundary. And that happens when you begin to stretch your box from within. That's exactly when you begin to live by design and become an authentic self leader at heart!

You then are naturally adventurous because you then know when to think out of the box, and when to get back into the box. You don't disturb. You rather create harmony.

And if you are asking me about the way to do it then you're asking me...

...How to Think Out of the Box?

Authentic self leaders break out of the patterns. To think out of the box is primarily to break out of the accepted patterns of reality. You need to undo what you acquired as perceptions and open up for different ones.

This is a two pronged process. Let's see what they are:

First Step: UNDO (Ctrl + Z)

Ask a farmer, "How important is fertility of soil for a good harvest?" and you'll get an answer, "It's an undeniable precondition for a good harvest."

Such is the need to UNDO your existing beliefs and make yourself available to the unknown.

How often have you heard your teacher, trainer, or boss asking you to think out of the box? How did you respond to it within?

You must've shouted in your head, "What the heck is this box?" or "How the hell am I going to think out of the box?"

Here's how: Don't think of answers straightaway.

On the opposite, reframe your questions. Seek answers to different questions. Instead of asking what's going to happen when I do this, you ask what this is for.

Boom! You feel the shift.

I hope I have your attention.

The first question you need to ask yourself to set the process in motion is this: Why must I think differently?

Begin with the question above because living in the box is easier that living out of the box. We have been trained and conditioned for it. Our family, friends, schools and society have trained us to conform. And conformity is living in the box. It is accepting things without raising questions.

As noted earlier, living out of the box is to stretch your limits. Living in the box is safer. You have a safety net. Living out of the box is challenging. You are in the wild.

People support you for conforming and any attempt to live out of the box is frowned upon. It's almost as if waging a war against an army of conformists.

Since you are here out of your own choice, you must be having the power of a strong 'why' behind your mission. Your strong cause in the form of 'why' makes you tough enough to persist.

The second question you need to ask yourself to continue is this: Which is the 'box' I intend to think out of?

Remember, this box which you have chosen to stretch the limits of is the limit of your thoughts.

Sadly, most of what we learn at schools is about how others have perceived life around, because most of our education has bombarded upon us how others saw, felt and experienced life. We, like sponge, have been absorbing all the information, knowledge, and experiences that others created for themselves.

The question is: were we ever trained to go beyond them?

I doubt.

So, we passively kept absorbing the imaginative limitations of knowledge. We were left to accept that 'that' was the furthest that could ever be discovered.

To think out of the box is to think like an artist, not like a painter. To become an authentic self leader is an art. And an artist is not bothered about the success of his masterpiece. He just is in love with what he is creating.

On the opposite, what the painter does is for a livelihood. Therefore, to think like an artist is to say, "It might not work. But still I am not bothered about it." That is the difference between a common achiever and an authentic self leader.

Now that you have chosen to think out of the box and live a life of self-reliance, self-efficacy and natural self-confidence, you must challenge the status quo. You must challenge the way you learnt to perceive life because only then you can...

Second Step: REDO (Ctrl + Y)

Get your spacesuit ready as we go skydiving. You're making a dive into the unknown. But isn't this what you committed to when you signed the self leadership pledge? Go back and read it again to install it permanently in your subconscious mind.

The very fact that you have come this far is a sure sign you are committed to self leadership. I appreciate your commitment.

So now that you are here, the question that might challenge you is this: How do I think out of the box?

Here's how you can: By developing the following qualities within:

1. Willingness to be wrong
2. Willingness to try the unknown
3. Willingness to risk
4. Willingness to see the BIG picture and
5. Willingness to be open-minded

What you will discover after quantum leaps into the unknown might be what you never expected. So don't be hasty in judging it right or wrong. Don't be hasty to rate it a success or a setback.

The secret is to accept that what you discovered is a new learning. It is a new way of looking at possibility. The moment you wake up to this new realization, there are no limits. You set your soul free!

What you just did was what millions fail to even think of?

Pat yourselves on the back!

You are a great one for challenges, aren't you?

So here's the big one for you...

...Explore the Creator Within?

""The only true wisdom is in knowing you know nothing" -
Socrates"

Universe always works through your creativity. Dig deep and you'll agree that your 'I Don't Know' approach comes from the desire to know and create more. You are designed to be curious, creative, and committed. You feel alive and in harmony when you turn a creator because you are in the flow.

On the opposite, the instant you stop being creative, you begin to decay and life turns mundane. You create more life and add value to life when your thoughts and actions originate from the spirit of 'I Don't Know'.

Somewhere in your heart, you are sure that there are better and creative ways to do things. Whether it's your finances, relationships, or self-improvement, the answer lies in the 'I Don't Know' domain. The trick is to build momentum. The faster you tap it, the quicker you get the results because the key to reinvent yourself is to stay curious and stay the course.

I want you to work like a heat-seeking missile and understand that you can take any action you want - as long as you are willing to accept the consequences of your choices. Because that's exactly how dreams are built.

So now, it's all yours to explore and you can begin your journey right now by asking yourself, "What don't I know?"

Way to go! High five!

Actionable Knowledge

Decide the next smallest action steps you decide to take to create a newer you:

1. _____
2. _____
3. _____

CHAPTER TWELVE

CREATE YOUR OWN 'AHA' MOMENTS

""The whole idea of motivation is a trap. Forget motivation. Just do it. Exercise, lose weight, test your blood sugar or whatever. Do it without motivation. And then, guess what? After you start doing the thing, that's when the motivation comes and makes it easy for you to keep on doing it."
- JOHN C. MAXWELL "

FROM THE YEAR 1998 to 2000, I kept waiting for my 'aha' moment so that I could feel inspired to work on my goals. I kept waiting for my supreme moment to take what Joe Vitale calls 'The Inspired Action'.

In desperation, I also began looking towards astrologers. While this bolstered up my wait for the moment, I kept urging them to decide an auspicious moment for me to start working on my ideas. Three years passed before I could blink. They vanished in front of my eyes before I realized that 'that' supreme moment would never come until I acted upon my calling.

The belief that had held me back was a thought impressed upon my mind by one of my astrologers through his words – "You must wait for three years before you take any action towards your purpose. That's when your good time starts."

The words kept me from taking any action.

It was as if he had implanted his idea in some invisible layers of my mind. It stuck in me and got me stuck.

Further, he also warned me that I would fail if I didn't heed his advice. This also got engraved in my mind. I internalized his opinions so strongly that millions of moments passed by before I woke up. I realized it very late that 'that' empowered moment is one which I act upon.

Such a moment can never be anytime else than 'now'.

I asked myself, "What decides the inspiration in the moment?" and got answer from within, "The inspiration in the moment comes from the value you choose to attribute to the moment. And this value comes from what you choose to do in the moment."

> "*"Never believe a prediction that doesn't empower you."*
> *-Sean Stephenson*"

Life of a moment depends on what you choose to do with it. What you choose to think and act in that moment decides how it is going to empower your life.

It's not the moment that does something to you. Rather, it's how you act upon it that decided the outcome.

Remember, you are the doer and you are the master!

Then what are 'moments'? They are just hollow capsules of time. And they pass by showering on you the opportunities for you to act upon. They are for you to fill your creative stuff with. Once you fill these hollow capsules with your action, you ignite the process of creation.

Authentic self leaders know that their inner value comes from what they do 'now' and what they choose to invest their time in.

Ultimately, the outcome of your life depends on the kind of stuff that you choose to fill these hollow capsules with.

The stuff you fill in the form first is your thought. It's your thought that begins to shape to that hollow capsule. And then you call it the moment of your life.

With this, the cycle of creation takes off.

What remains is building momentum.

And Here's what you can do to infuse...

...Movement into Moment

Ever wondered how the process of creation begins?

It begins with the thoughts we project into the capsule. Our thought becomes the source stuff for our creation.

There are two kinds of thoughts you can choose from and set the process of creation in motion.

1. Thoughts about things you would NOT love to experience.
2. Thoughts about things you would love to experience.

All experiences in your life are a result of your choice. They belong from either of the above mentioned kinds.

When you constantly project thoughts about things which you would not like to manifest, you unconsciously pump life-force into those thoughts. Thus you keep attracting more of such stuff with compounded and magnified force.

When you project thoughts like, "I hate to waste time" you will actually find yourselves stuck meaninglessly to the idiot box. And then you find yourself waiting for your inspired moment to arrive and motivate you to act. Interesting!

You sit with newspapers stacking piles of negative information in your mind and keep expecting the results to be positive. Have you ever considered what a colossal wastage of human potential this is?

Imagine if time were to come into your life in the form of empty capsules. What would you name them as? If it were me, I would name them as 'NOW'. These moments obey you only when YOU take charge to fill them. Each time a new empty capsule is born it brings you a fresh opportunity to act upon.

The question is how you can make these empty capsules get you a life of choice.

Here's how: When you fill such empty capsules with the thoughts about things you would love to experience, you attract more of such positive experiences.

In front of your eyes you begin to develop ideas to create what you want in life. This is how you begin to take your baby steps towards the direction of your goal.

And that's how you begin to put movement into moment.

Your NOW is when you choose to act. NOW is when you can dare to take your baby step towards making your desire come true. This one step then gives you the much needed confidence. It fills you with motivation enough to take the next step, and then one more and then you begin taking strides to success.

Hurray!

A hundred such infant steps can build momentum enough to keep you going until each moment transforms into an empowered moment.

This is how you materialize your desire.

This is how you create what you want.

Finally, can you have a jungle without dangerous animals looming large? And that's why you also need to...

...Be Wary of the Tricky Trap

"People say motivation doesn't last. Neither does bathing – that's why we recommend it daily."
– Zig Ziglar

Here's the most dangerous one for us – Waiting for the 'aha' moment. It is a self-damaging thought-habit. It is shirking off our responsibility towards action. We turn you a shirker. Each time we say we are waiting for our empowered moment, we disregard the moment at hand and consider it worthless and ineffective.

Thus, we leave everything that has to happen on 'future time'.

Remember, time is a resource. Action does not emerge from resource. It originates from our resourcefulness. It doesn't come from time. It comes from our attitude towards time. We build our attitude towards time from the way we perceive our life.

To wait for an empowered moment is to dissipate the natural reserves of life energy on absolutely nothing.

In doing so, we actually tend to fill time with worthless achievements and toxic temporary goals.

Such a thought-habit lessens our chances of growing a self leadership mindset. Take it from me - a self leadership mindset is an important prerequisite to a fulfilled life.

And let me also make clear that all external achievements that we equate with success are things that we chase to get happiness. It is happiness that we crave for in the forms of products, positions, and possessions.

Matt Killingsworth in his famous TED talk on "Happiness" offered us a wonderful formula for happiness. His research done through 'trackyourhappiness.org' on the relationship between mind wandering and happiness brought amazing results into lime light.

Over 15000 people from over 80 countries participated in his survey with a whopping 650,000 real time reports. And the results were explosive.

They proved scientifically that people were happier when they were focused on the present moment. Above all, unhappiness was found to be linked to mind-wandering.

And what's more, the result had nothing to do with whether you loved the task at hand or not. What mattered was whether you were focused on the present moment or not.

So the study proves beyond any doubt that focus is the way to flow. As a consequence, an authentic self leader accepts each moment as a potent resource with infinite possibilities. By developing such a mindset we learn to set our expectations to something new. We begin to treat life as a series of knocks to be answered. Whether we add misery to it or joy is our personal choice.

The single most important point is that as a self leader we look at each moment as a seed. Such mindset if used resourcefully, nourished with 'possibility thoughts', has the potential to bear millions of fruits called achievements. That's it.

And then we stop chasing achievements.

Rather, we begin to appreciate the power within.

At the same time, turning the seed into an achievement depends on the value we attach to it.

We can do it successfully only when we learn how to...

...Tap The Inner GPS

Listen inwards – that's the only way you can get to your goal. Listen to your inner call. I would take it a step deeper and say, "This is the only way god speaks with you." Call it your gut feel or intuition or call, it is how universe responds to your questions.

"When you talk, you are only repeating what you already know. But if you listen, you may learn something new," said Dalai Lama.

Each job I took initially, I would know in my gut that this isn't it... this isn't it... this isn't it. I might not have been able to put the entire picture together. However I knew there was something better yet to show up.

You too must have experienced such feelings. You get such experiences when you get attuned to your inner voice. Start trusting your intuition. I would rather call it activating your emotional GPS. It's your super-conscious talking to you through another dimension. Why don't you just go deeper and tap this power of your own super-conscious? You can do this with guaranteed results by trusting your gut feel.

Put aside at least 2 hours a week to spend in solitude. Allow your mind to chatter. And you will begin to hear the voice within. Just keep listening. Pay attention to what resonates deep down and you can fuel the fire of transformation from within the moment you start acknowledging them. Remember you are not here for sprint. You are here for a marathon – a lasting impact.

Friends, this is when your 'aha-moment' happens to you. Remember, it's part of the process. It is a means to an end. It is not something you wait for. It happens when you are functioning synchronistic manner - aligned from inside. It happens only when you are willing to listen to life in silence. It happens only when you allow life to flow through you non-judgmentally. Rather you become life!

That is exactly when you begin enjoying your journey from...

...Mind to Matter

Want to turn an alchemist? Let's see how you can turn your ideas real. It's now a reality that possibility lies in how we attend to the moment at hand because we actually fill our moments with our mind.

In essence, our life is made of mind-stuff.

Most quantum physicists believe there is no universe without the observer. Then we have a possibility only when WE acknowledge one.

Mind-bending!

What each moment brings to us is an opportunity. It is for us to execute our choice. We live like a 'Master of Our Fate' by choosing to fill life into the moment. Else we end up a 'Slave of Our Destiny'.

What you do with the moment is your choice. Either you make the best of the unlimited resource, or make a colossal wastage of universal energy. It all depends upon you.

Decide now to make the best use of your mental powers. Choose to create your life. Surviving is easy. It is natural. It is instinctual. But creating a life you desire is a choice. This is the only way you can exercise your right to be human because this is the only capacity that differentiates you from all other species.

This brings us to the most crucial element linked to your present – your decision. It's crucial to your success. Whether you wake up at a predetermined time every morning or leave it to chance, whether you use your 'will' for your goals or diffuse it pursuing worthless things is a matter of YOUR choice.

1. What kind of job do you wish to do?
2. What project do you desire to start up?
3. What do you want to write a book about?
4. Which car do you dream to drive?
5. What's the house you see your loved ones in?

All that you dream of being, doing, and having depends on how you answer this question: What do you choose to do with the moment in hand?

Because...

NOW is the moment of POWER!

NOW is the moment of CHOICE!

NOW is the moment of CREATION!

Once you acknowledge this, you can achieve everything you have ever dreamed of. You can create everything you have ever wished for. You can do most things in life which millions don't even dare to dream of.

The key is to know it's not about what toys you collect in the end. What matters is who you become as a result of this process.

Once you begin to put into use the power of choice into practice, you will begin to see magical transformation in your life. People around you will be amazed at the speed at which you will reach your goals. You might even begin to secretly take delight in surprising people by the rate at which you accomplish success.

The simple truth is you don't have to wait for your aha-moments. You can create as many as you wish for. And this can happen only when you act on your ideas.

NO EXCUSES.

Finally, your inspired moment is NOW!

And your fate is something you choose now or lose now!

So pay close attention to your inner voice. Let the invisible power guide you from within. Change happens when you know that you are capable of choosing your life, and when you are courageous enough to let your higher self guide you.

And that is when your 'aha-moments' start showing up.

Imagine as if these aha-moments were comets filled with magical powers flying across the sky. The only way you can draw the magical power from them is by following this *two- step system*:

1. Listen to your inner voice.
2. Keep acting upon it.

Once you put them into practice, you will see some real change soon. Do them and create your own 'aha' moments in life.

So what are you waiting for? Excited to live your dreams? You probably are asking, "When's the right moment?"

"Of course now!"

Yes, NOW is your inspired moment. Now is your empowered moment. Believe you me, NOW is the most creative moment of your life!

Take a pen and start re-scripting your story!

I know your brain is craving for more.

Wait until you reach 'Explore Meaning Through Time' in 'You.2 – A Crash Course In Authentic Self Leadership' to get the insider knowledge on squeezing the best value out of time.

For now, just be here, listen to your gut, and ACT on it!

Actionable Knowledge

Decide the next smallest action steps you decide to take to create a newer you:

1. _____
2. _____
3. _____

CHAPTER THIRTEEN

GRAB THE MASTER KEY: PERCEPTION TO REALITY

""Reality is merely an illusion, albeit a very persistent one"
-Albert Einstein "

WOW! WE HAVE COME a long way! But what you will absorb from this chapter will help you upshift to the next level altogether.

Stop and look at things around. What do you see?

The same objects which you must have seen hundreds of times? Now choose one object specifically and focus on it. The more you focus on it the more it would get brighter and clearer. Change your position and look at it from another angle. I am sure you will certainly notice newer details.

Julian Beever, the world-renowned pavement artist, uses the 'trick of the eye' and 'anamorphosis' techniques to influence perception. The masterpiece he creates needs you to look at them from a particular viewpoint, or with a camera which he arranges on a tripod for you to see.

Like the illusion Julian creates, our minds tend to fill in the details of something it either thinks it understands or is yet to know fully. This is fine until you allow it for the sake of the fun of doing it. However, wandering through life allowing everyone around to create your perceptions is a sure-fire way to a fully dissatisfied life.

As a child, you arrived as an alien into the world around. But the world was just as alien for you. You were a perfectly clean bio-computer not even having a separate self-concept for the first 18 months because you and your mother were almost one. You were yet to form your identity.

You offered yourself as a blank canvas to be splashed colors of experiences upon. Most part of your experience of life as a child was limited to oscillating between pain and pleasure.

Gradually you were exposed to the impressions from outside and you began downloading information, programs, and ideas from outside. And that's when you began to build your self-concept.

Once you started interpreting the incidents happening around, you started weaving your own story. You did it time after time by finding inspiration from people around. People around you started defining you by identifying what you like and what you dislike, what you enjoy and what you don't, what you look good in and what doesn't suit you, you are this one and you are that one... etc.

In most cases, it was your parents, grandparents, neighbors, peer group and lately our constant companion – television, who trained you to make meanings out of experiences.

You were almost two when you began to speak your 'I' statements for the first time – I am this, I like this, I want that... etc. You made meanings from incidents taking cue from others. You started making conscious choices as you gradually grew to become adolescents.

While most of us just wanted to use our right to make a choice, some of us were successful at making informed choices.

You must understand the fact that we drift across life thinking we are living our story. It's when we realize that this isn't the life we wanted to live, we find ourselves stuck.

What is the story you are living? Who wrote it? Did you consciously choose to create it? If not, what's stopping you from changing it? Do you seriously intend to change it once and for all? If you really intend to do it, you must take up the reins of your life.

And that's how you begin your...

...Conscious Creation

> *"Whatever the result, we make decisions based on a perception of the world that may not, in fact, be completely accurate."*
> *-Simon Sinek*

Now that you are thinking like an achiever, let's spend some time studying how you can become a creator. First let's go back to roots: Each time you understood a certain incident in a certain way; you formed a perception of that incident in your minds. You understood it in a certain way as your conscious choice. And the repetitions etched them on your behavior.

As it continued, such perceptions started re-creating more of such incidents in our lives and we named it – FATE.

Now focus here. This is a small yet the most important section, which can give you the juice of this book. So pay close attention.

You consciously contribute to personal evolution when you make a conscious attempt to alter your perception.

It's more in a fashion of adjusting the lens of your camera for a better view. It helps you make your purpose clearer, add value to your life, and create meaning out of it.

> *""What we see mainly depends on what we look for."*
> *--John Lubbock"*

As you become aware of this factor, you keep changing how you perceive the world around, yourself, and what happens to you. All this happens because of your conscious interaction with the world around.

Your perception of what happens to you helps you:

1. Choose your response to the stimulus
2. Choose your action-step
3. Instill the drive within to persist till you see change

All that you allow yourself to accept as your perceptions shape who you are and also the way you are going to experience life around. The very fact that you have been with me so far proves you have an innate desire to create a better a perception of life. I appreciate your burning desire to create a better self-concept. Because you now know that your self-concept is the software which runs your life.

All you need to do is to take care of your ...

...Self-Image

Your self-image is a glimpse of what your future holds for you. The image of your 'self' that you visualize now becomes your reality in future. The probability of your self-image becoming a self-fulfilling prophecy is higher because it is you who consciously choose to project the image. And that's how you become the co-creator of your fate.

It's as if the whole universe conspires to materialize what you projected in the form of self-image. It is as if some unknown force is at work materializing your image.

The question is how do you change your reality?

Here's the...

...Question You Must Ask

On most occasions, you tend to be harder upon yourself than you are on others. You spend more time thinking about what all you cannot do instead of what's possible.

Fallacies of society become your realities overtime. The right question to check the self-defeating thoughts and self-sabotaging perception within is, "Would I want to turn these self-defeating thoughts real?"

If your answer is NO, then I welcome you to change your reality instantly.

And here are simple ways you can employ to do it:

1. Choose better books to read.
2. Choose better friends to hang out with.
3. Choose better audios to listen to.
4. Choose better videos to watch.
5. Choose to do everything that will help you stretch your comfort zone.

Finally, if life is an illusion why don't you choose a better one? Change what you see to change what you get because undeniably you are the... ...The Master Illusionist!

Have a plan?

Actionable Knowledge

Decide the next smallest action steps you decide to take to create a newer you:

1. _____
2. _____
3. _____

CHAPTER FOURTEEN

THERE'S NO PLAN; AND THAT OK!

"Life is what happens to you while you are busy making other plans."
– John Lennon "

TO SOME, DECEMBER 31st is just another weekday or weekend night. The calendar finishes out and the year increases by another notch, but other than accidentally writing the previous year for the next few weeks nothing really changes.

For others, the New Year means a sort of fresh start. It is a time where many of us will reflect on the achievements and struggles of our last year. And look forward to the next year with an idea of what we would like to accomplish.

New job? New home? New habit? And everywhere you turn there are quick and easy guides to help you accomplish those goals. Articles such as "Five Steps to Winning in the new year!" and "Get Your Dream Job With These 3 Easy Tricks" will be posted to social media, flashed in magazines, and discussed on daytime talk shows.

But life isn't like that, is it?

We like to treat life like a recipe, believing that if we follow the steps and use the right ingredients, the end product will be just what we hoped. The problem with that is that the world is wild, unpredictable, unstable, and surprising.

Life makes no promises. And there is no one correct way to accomplish your goals for this year. You can have a strategy that is specific, attainable, and realistic. But that does not mean your plan will result in success.

The key to becoming an authentic self leadership is not in the plans you make or in having the perfect process. The key to meeting your goals, simply put, is you. You are your greatest force for good in life. You are the only one that will determine outcome of this year in your life.

What you plan might not succeed but the outcome would certainly be a learning experience. If learning is your goal then you can never fail. This should not in any way discourage you from planning your life.

Remember, all preparation is to prepare you for the unexpected.

Here's the good news: When your intention is sincere, life mostly surprises you with results better than you had asked for. And most of the times these surprises are results of the empowering questions you ask yourself.

So what are those...

...Empowering Questions

"Unless commitment is made, there are only promises and hopes; but no plans"
– Peter F.Drucker

How do we make sure this year is everything you dreamed? I don't have a series of keys or tips for you.

Instead, I have a few questions to help you realize your own potential this year.

And they are:

- What is the belief you wish to be an epitome of?
- What is your major purpose?
- What do you want the most important people in your life to remember you for?
- What do you really want out of your life?
- Is it a steady a job with fair pay, or a meaningful life?
- What does your future look like?

Now write it down. Make it real. Tell someone you trust. This is your motivation, the fuel in your tank, and the hope that will power your adventure.

If you believe it's true, it's also important is to find out how to tap the power of questions so that you can unleash the self leader within and live an internally driven life.

But before you do that, you will want to get inside the ways questions can impact you.

Here's how they impact you: They give you orientation. They help you focus. They help you set your direction but they go further.

What most people don't realize is they give you orientation in three ways:

1. **Thought Orientation**
2. **Time Orientation**
3. **Speed Orientation**

1. *Thought Orientation:* The questions you ask yourselves turn your perspective pessimistic, optimistic, or proactive. Therefore, it's just not enough to say that you think positive. Step ahead and choose those questions which will lead to thoughts you would want to play around with. That's when you see change.
2. *Time Orientation:* The questions you put to yourselves make your perspective past oriented, present oriented, or future-focused. So it's just not enough to say that you think positive. Step ahead and decide to select the questions which will help you accept your past, empower your present and create a better future. That's how you create the future you wish to experience.
3. *Speed Orientation:* The kind of questions you ask yourselves also decide what speed you will move towards our goals at. So instead of just being satisfied with "When will I do?" Why don't you step further and ask, "How soon must I act upon my intention?" Because that's how you decide the speed at which you see change.

Ready to jet off to your dream life? Here's the....

...The Next Big Truth

"*"It is not good enough for things to be planned – they still have to be done; for the intention to become a reality, energy has to launched*

into operation."
– Walt Kelly "

Goals are not meant to replace the life we already have. They are meant to be the next chapter in the story we are already living.

While we cannot control everything that happens – we all have chapters we would like to go back and rewrite. We can certainly control how we respond to those challenges. Let the good times build gratitude for what we have accomplished, and the difficult times fuel our desire for a self-empowered life.

The next question is probably the most difficult.

And the one that requires the greatest amount of honesty and self-evaluation: How hard are you willing to work to reach your goal?

Don't answer this one too quickly. How many hours do you think Mohammad Ali must have spent in practice? How many hours do you think Sania Mirza, Saina Nehwal or P. V. Sindhu spend on the court each week? How many hours do you think legendary actors like Kamal Haasan put in every day?

You must set the level of your intention because no one can do it for you. Want to be the CEO of a company? The most sought-after expert in your field? Your goals are waiting for you to accomplish them, and you are the most powerful force in making them come true.

So now you have a dream, and you are willing to work for it.

...Now what?

" *"Set a goal, and in small, consistent steps, work to reach it. Get support from your peers when you start flagging. Repeat. You will change."*
– Seth Godin "

Take just one next step toward your goal. That's your immediate goal. There's no trick here. Your mindset is more important than any technique. Just keep moving forward. There will be roadblocks and hazards all along the way. But that's just drama that will make your story all the more entertaining in the end. Make mistakes. Stumble. Suffer failure. Just keep moving forward. Success is inevitable.

And when people ask how you did it, you can tell them honestly that you simply chased your dream, and made the most of your journey along the way.

Surprisingly, it becomes far easier when you tap the...

...The Power of Action

One of the most remarkable discoveries in 20th century success research is the role of ACTION in your personal development. Why don't we first begin with defining action?

To me, action can be defined as something with a consequence. Going by this definition, even inaction can be considered an action.

Why? Because inaction or failure to act on our part also has a noticeable consequence that can dramatically impact our life.

For instance, a person who fails to take action towards goal, or fails to read regularly, or to listen to positive audio tapes, and attend training programs and seminars, or anything that he needs to do to reach his goals, is actually committing to "inaction."

The consequences are obvious. By the very fact that it has devastating consequences on one's future, it certainly can be considered an action. The crucial actions that determine the quality of your life turn around the virtues and values that you decide to accept in your life. The reality is they are as important to your physical life as is breathing.

The secret to draw happiness from action is to sync them with your values.

Point to remember: What you value most determines what you do.

The trick is when you act in alignment with your values, you feel good about yourself. And when you get misaligned with your values, you feel badly about yourself. Your values act as your internal compass to help you correct your course each time you get distracted.

And here's something you'll find useful each time you decide to focus. Get ready to tap the...

...The Secret Source

All power to act on your ideas emerges from the source called INTENTION. All those who seem to be taking action towards their goals with effortless grace, draw their power from this potent source.

Mere wants and wishes do not fuel your desire enough to build the required momentum. To gain the desirable momentum you must turn the desire in your heart into a powerful intention. And then you experience a major shift. You become a channel to a mystical force that propels you towards taking the action you need to take. You begin to crystallize your thoughts into matter. You suddenly start seeing your dreams as possible and actionable. That's exactly what you need to see success. You ignite the process of creation by turning your wishes into intentions and then you are ready to...

...Give Wings to Your Desires

Imagine you have all the resources in the world provided and success guaranteed. Now take a note pad and a pen and list 100 of your heart's desires for the next 10 years in exactly one hour.

Prune the list to the most significant 25.

Choose the top 10 of them and finally

Choose one that if you materialize would realize the rest of your goals.

That is going to be Your Major Goal for the next ten years. All you need to do is stick to the easy structure you'll get in the companion copy of this book – "You.2 – A Crash Course In Authentic Self Leadership" and make your journey remarkable.

Grab your copy now and join the thousands who built what you have been dreaming for.

Go on!

Co-create Your Life!

Actionable Knowledge

Decide the next smallest action steps you decide to take to create a newer you:

1. _____

2. _____

3. _____

Author

Ranjan Kumar

Ranjan Kumar is the Founder, Bestselling Author, and Authentic Self Leadership Coach at Mysticfusion International. He is an ardent student of life on a mission of helping 100000 people discover the self leader within and live a life of self-reliance, self-efficacy and natural self-confidence.

He conducts transformational seminars on personal leadership and is an acclaimed transformational speaker for educational and corporate groups in India.

The Top Outstanding National Trainer Awardee for Junior Chamber International India – South – 2015 is a Certified Transformational Coach who considers helping people make meaning his purpose.

Most importantly he is fired-up every moment to sync himself with his purpose. To learn more about him visit:

www.mysticfusion.in

"The illiterate of the 21st century will not be those who cannot read and write, but those who cannot learn, unlearn, and relearn."

-Alvin Toffler

Printed in the USA
CPSIA information can be obtained
at www.ICGtesting.com
LVHW091233131223
766027LV00062B/1495

9 781637 457313